sunday roast

the complete guide to
cooking and carving

clarissa dickson wright
and johnny scott

with photography by gus filgate

sunday roast

the complete guide to
cooking and carving

kyle books

To Mollypop who taught her daughter always to order four ribs when three would do and to Walter who carved so beautifully and passed his skill on to his son

This edition published in 2007 by Kyle Books,
an imprint of Kyle Cathie Limited
www.kylecathie.com

Hardcover published in Great Britain in 2002 by Headline Book Publishing

ISBN 978 1 904920 68 7

10 9 8 7 6 5 4 3 2 1

Designer Geoff Hayes
Photography Gus Filgate & Kate Whitaker
Home Economist Nicole Szabason
Stylist Penny Markham
Production Sha Huxtable & Alice Holloway

Library of Congress Control Number: 2007928166

Color reproduction by SC (Sang Choy) International Pte Ltd
Printed in Singapore by Star Standard Industries

All photography by Gus Filgate except pages 2, 6, 10, 13, 17, 31, 147, 154 by Kate Whitaker
Illustrations: page 37, The Cottesmore Prize Heifer, Giles, James William; page 57, A Prize Sheep of the Old Lincoln Breed, Adamson, W.: page 81, A Pig in its Sty, Fox, E.M; all courtesy of Bridgeman Art Library

contents

introduction:
johnny scott

The seed of the idea for this book was planted at a lunch party in January 2001. The centerpiece was a magnificent, well-hung, 13 pounds (6 kg.) wing rib of beef, oozing blood and showing the sort of fat cover and meat marbling that is only possible, in these days of post-BSE government restrictions, with one of the traditional slow-maturing native breeds. A side of beef, enough to feed twelve people with plenty left over, is a thing of beauty and, naturally, the roast was the focal point of conversation. As I carved happily, the damage to our culture caused by the socialist policy of importing cheap foreign food, became a topic of discussion.

Before the fast-food phenomen of the 1960s, virtually every household bought a piece of meat from their local butcher, large enough to feed the family on Sunday and provide meals for most of the following week. As supermarkets dominated consumer buying, eating habits changed and gratitude for food, expressed by the convention of Sunday lunch, ceased in many households. The art of carving became, by and large, lost to the generations that followed.

It is hard to believe that anything constructive could have resulted from BSE, still less the shambles over the handling of foot and mouth disease, yet the effect has been to make consumers ask where their food is coming from and to demand traceable, healthy commodities. There is now a long overdue swing back toward traditional family values and appreciation for home-grown, domestic produce. This has been reflected in the popularity of farmers' markets, "Q" Guild butchers, and the growth in organic farming. Quality products are increasingly accessible, but what is lacking for many people are the forgotten arts of cooking proper roasts and, just as important, how to carve them.

introduction:
clarissa dickson wright

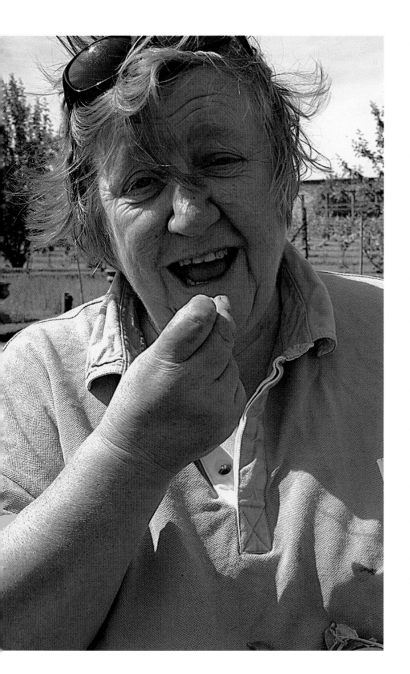

Having no family of my own, I am welcomed as an honorary aunt into many houses, and in these visitings it is brought home to me how important is the ritual of the family meal. For my own part I would have known nothing of my family, being as I am so much the youngest, except for sitting down at a table with them. I wonder at those families whose members grab their portions like animals and slink off to televisions and their own rooms to gnaw at them without social graces conversations or manners. Those who think it doesn't matter forget that social skills have to be learned: Conversation flows at mealtimes, people learn how to eat properly, and how to enjoy food.

I have noticed over the decades how much better skilled in the real world are those children who learned their skills around the meal table than those who had to learn them as adults, and at the end of the day it is these skills that help one to get on in life, to win jobs, lovers, and friends. If you are one who objects that your children find it dull, perhaps you should examine whether you take the trouble to include them and to exchange points of view, or whether the food you serve them is appealing. If you cry, "It's too much trouble," why did you have them in the first place? Since September 11, 2001, there has been a greater feeling of wasted family occasions and comings-together, as if that terrible tragedy brought home how little time we all spend with each other.

There is no easier way to feed a lot of people than with a roast, and we hope this book will help you on that path.

a few principles concerning cooking and carving

Many things affect the cooking and carving of meat other than the right recipe and a sharp knife. The age of the animal, the breed, feed, and hanging are all vital, as is the most basic understanding of the beast you are about to work with. If you know a little about the structure of the meat, and how it changes with age, you will be a better cook and indeed a better carver.

All animal meat is muscle. The more mature the muscle, the coarser the meat and the longer it will need to be cooked to tenderize it. Young animals—lambs and calves, for instance—will have less developed musculature than an older sheep or steer, so the meat will be more tender in cooking. (However, lacking the fat of older animals, they will often also lack flavor, and will cook dry.)

Apart from maturity, the more a muscle is worked, the coarser the meat will be. The most hardworking parts of any grazing animal are the locomotive parts—the neck, chest, shoulders, and legs—and the meat will again need long slow cooking to tenderize it. The parts of the animal that are least worked are the back, loin, and rump—the parts farthest from hoof and horn—and it is from there that the prime cuts come that can be roasted.

The same is true to an extent of poultry. The older a chicken, the longer it will need to cook to become tender. Because the legs are the hardest-working parts of flightless birds such as domestic chickens and turkeys, they are tougher in texture than the relatively immobile breasts, and often need longer cooking. And the meat of poultry legs is darker too because of the oxygen stored in frequently used muscles. This explains why the breast flesh of game birds can be as dark as the legs: they spend far more time working their wings, thus their breasts, in flight.

Fish proteins are not the same as those of land animals and birds. The muscles are arranged in different patterns, which is why fish can cook—and fall apart—so quickly.

Meat needs hanging to tenderize it, to allow the muscles to relax and the flavor to mature. While a beef carcass hangs, for instance, the fibers of the meat start to break down. This involves shrinkage, of course, but it also greatly improves flavor and tenderness when cooked. Supermarket meat is never hung because this process allows the meat to shrink. Pay more to a butcher and let it shrink in his cold storerather than in your oven. The same thing applies to game. When newly shot, most game birds are fairly bland in flavor, but hanging will both tenderize the meat and give it its characteristic gamey flavor.

Actually, one of the most important elements in successful cooking and carving is a reliable butcher or poulterer! Not only will he have chosen and bought the right carcasses, but he will also have hung them for the requisite time. Often he will also have prepared the roast as he should—chining a rib roast, for instance—which assists both cook and carver. And never forget that meat kept and cooked on the bone is sweeter, juicier and more full of flavor.

We should say a few general words on the principles of roasting. Dorothy Hartley, the scholar-gypsy, wrote that when they closed the door on the ovens of England, they ruined roasting. We think that is a little harsh. Roasting is the method of cooking meat by direct heat. It is most normal to place the meat in a hot oven to seal it, or to do this as a separate process and then cook the meat more gently for the remainder of its time. Only prime cuts of meat can be roasted successfully: In the fast heat of roasting, the coarser muscle fibers of less prime parts would not have time to break down and become tender. The meat must either be self-basted with its own fat or, if very dry, covered with extra fat. Meat needs fat for flavor and digestibility, and don't let anyone tell you different.

And the less prime and older cuts of meat, poultry, and game often need to be roasted in an entirely different way. Pot roasting means the meat is put with flavorings and some liquid in a covered container, either on top of the stove or in the oven, where it partially bakes and partially steams over the much longer time required to tenderize it. Although not classified as prime cuts, these "lesser" parts of the animal, because they contain more fat, often contain much more flavor.

It is usually recommended that a roast or bird is allowed to "rest" after it is taken out of the oven, and this is important. If meat or a chicken were to be carved straight out of the oven, the flesh would be rubbery and the juices would pour out. The heat left within the meat will continue to cook it slightly while resting, but it will also allow the temperature throughout the meat to equalize, and the juices to be equally distributed. This makes the meat much easier to carve, and all the juices will be deliciously retained.

carving

"We are always in pain for a man, who instead of cutting up a fowl genteelly is hacking for half an hour across a bone, greasing himself and besplattering the company with sauce: but where the master of a table dissects a bone with ease and grace, he is not only well thought of, but admired."

Thus wrote the Reverend John Trusler in his opus *The Honours of the Table* (1788), which included a section on the "Art of Carving." Trusler was writing at a time when a thorough knowledge of carving was considered an important part of both every young gentleman's and lady's education, and carving knives were used daily. This was an age when the roast reigned supreme and "made" dishes were not considered a main course. As a universal household accomplishment, carving persisted until the 1950s. Since then convenience foods, the price of meat, and the ever-increasing pressures of modern living—particularly where both parents work—have produced a generation that is largely ignorant of the art. If Trusler was lamenting standards in 1788, Lord knows what he would make of the situation today.

How often have we seen the ambience of a dinner party evaporate as paterfamilias wrestles with a piece of meat, purchased for that special occasion. Face livid with humiliation and blaming his knife for being blunt, he saws ineptly while his anguished wife flits to and fro with a fixed grin as vegetables and gravy grow cold. All too often, when guests are bidden to dinner where roast meat, game, or poultry make up the main dish, the head of the household desperately tries to find someone else to do the carving. It is at times such as this, when the buck reaches me, that I am eternally grateful to my father. With infinite patience he dispelled much of the inhibiting myth attached to carving, and taught me to acquire a simple skill that is both practical and fun.

I treasure the memories of veritable festivity that was attached to the Sunday lunches of my childhood. When the meat had been delivered from the kitchen, my father would open the black, oblong, leather-covered case containing his carving knives. There, nestling in red satin, were two sets of Victorian knives, forks, and sharpening steels with stag's horn handles mounted with silver ferrules. Too precious to be immersed in soapy water with the rest of the silver, they were wiped with a damp cloth and the blades rubbed with olive oil. As children, we were never allowed to open the case and touch them lest sticky fingers marked the soft Sheffield steel. Selecting the appropriate combination (the larger for meat, the smaller for poultry), and stroking the blade briskly on the steel, he would say, "Now, John, attend me closely. If your knife is sharp, the meat properly cooked, and you keep your head, you cannot go wrong." These are the three maxims for successful carving.

a short history of carving

Historically, carving as an artistic accomplishment has a literature all of its own, and such was the importance given to the minutiae of the table in feudal times, that a *Boke of Kervinge* was printed by Wykynd de Worde, Caxton's successor, at the beginning of the sixteenth century. This was in an era when precious few books, apart from religious ones, were being printed. It is an indication of the esteem in which food was held during those uncertain times, when the risk of famine, drought, or pestilence meant a scarcity of food for all, that the role of man the hunter-gatherer, distributing the fruits of his labours to his dependants, was elevated to become part of the code of chivalry. Carvers in royal and noble households were actually aristocrats of lesser rank. Before the honor of knighthood was granted, a period of the noviciate had to be spent as a Carving Esquire and the terminology and observances, equally as complicated as those of venery, painstakingly learned. For instance, venison might not be touched by either hand, and only the left used to handle beef and mutton or to lift birds by their legs.

This was in an age when, apart from a few domestic animals kept mainly for milk, wool, and as beasts of burden, the main food source was derived from practically everything that ran, flew, or swam—from minnows to porpoises, sparrows to bustards, and all beasts of venery, chase, and warren except the wolf, fox, and marten. Each had to be carved according to rigid individual specification based on their standing in the codes of hunting. Herons, therefore, were dismembered, mallards unbraced, and cranes displayed. Geese were reared, swans lifted, and plovers minced. Bitterns were unjointed, curlews allayed. Woodcock, pigeons, and smaller birds were thighed, but partridges and quail winged. Hens were spoiled, capons sauced, and chickens "frusshed." Lucky chickens. Deer were broken, and the exact spot to begin carving a whole roast was governed by elaborate rules. Slices carved from the larger beasts had to be presented on a broad-bladed serving carver, cut into four, and held together by the fatty top strip. This acted as a handle, to be tossed to the dogs once the individual pieces had been gnawed off. There were at least twenty different ways of carving fish. Pike were splatted, barbels tusked, eels traunsened, lampreys sprung, and crabs tamed. Sturgeons were traunched, but a porpoise undertraunched.

Elaborate feasting was very much a part of medieval life. One of the more spectacular banquets took place when George Nevill (to whom "manners maketh man" is attributed) was installed as Archbishop of York in 1466. At a continuous sitting several days, he and his cronies scoffed their way through eighty oxen, six wild bulls, 1,004 sheep, 300 calves, 2,000 pigs, and 400 harts, bucks, and does, as well as a multitude of wildfowl, waders, partridges, pheasants, and little songbirds. With an amazing range of sea, river, and still-water fish were eight seals and four porpoises. God help any pages unfortunate enough to commit the social solecism of carving any of these the wrong way.

maintaining the edge

You cannot begin to carve unless your knives are properly sharp. Many a jolly family gathering has been ruined by a blunt knife. Modern carbon or stainless steel knives have sharp, factory ground blades which retain their edge almost indefinitely. An old set of steel knives discovered in an attic or acquired from an antique shop will need professional sharpening. Here, your friendly local butcher will almost certainly oblige with his electronic grinding stone. Thereafter, with both modern and old knives, the edge is maintained with the steel. Many people have been put off carving by the dexterity which professional chefs, butchers, and slaughtermen display when maintaining the edge of their knives. "I could never do that," we say, watching in awe as the blade flashes backward and forward on either side of the steel. You don't have to. These people use their knives all day and every day. One morning's knife work for them will equate to five years for the average carver.

Using a steel is very easy indeed, because you are not sharpening the knife, merely maintaining its edge. Take the steel in your left hand or vice versa if you are right-handed. Place the point on something that will protect the wood, on the edge of your sideboard. With the steel held level with the top of the sideboard, place your knife with the sharp side of the blade toward you, with the handle a couple of inches up from the tip of the steel. Holding the knife at an angle of 25 degrees to the steel, stroke it in a half circle toward you. This covers the whole length of the blade. Do this gently a few times, then turn the knife over and move the handle to the top of the steel and stroke away from you. There is something very soothing about this. Old steel makes a lovely tinkling sound, and it gives the carver a moment or two to study his piece of meat before setting to work.

the tools of the trade

If raising the art of carving and the intricacies of the hunting field to being part of the code of chivalry was an expression of gratitude for food on the table, the same is true of the utensils that were used. Cutlers were craftsmen of the same stature as jewelers and master armorers. In museums exquisite examples of workmanship can be seen from the Middle Ages in the form of carving knives with handles made from materials more associated with jewelery and religious artefacts. Delicately carved and sculpted in ivory, polished bone, horn, wood, and brass, and inlaid with amber, agate, silver, and lapis lazuli, they reflect the reverence attached to the ceremony of the table. During the following three centuries, when banquets became increasingly elaborate and magnificent, the cutler's art thrived. Implements of great beauty were created as new and more exotic materials were discovered: rock crystal, cornelian, aventurine, glass, coral, silver inlaid with niello and, of course, gold. Mother-of-pearl, porcelain, and faience are only some of the materials and combinations of material that have survived to give us an inkling of the glorious pageantry that was part of our forefathers' celebration of their grub.

Cutlery became less elaborate during the twentieth century, but a set of carvers remained the centerpiece of every bride's display of wedding gifts until the 1970s. Now it is very difficult to find anything remotely resembling the craftsmanship that existed when carving was at least a weekly occurrence in most households.

Let us look at what the aspiring carver is going to need, bearing in mind that his or her efforts will be something of a public demonstration. A certain amount of thought needs to be put into selecting knives that are going to complement the occasion. Basically you need a set of carvers, knives with curved points, one 12 inches (30cm.) long for bigger birds (geese and turkeys) and larger joints, the other 10 inches (25cm.) long for game birds, chickens, and small joints. A 10 inch (25cm.) long flexible ham knife, and a knife with a straight, round-ended blade 1 inch (2.5cm.) wide and 10 inches (25cm.) long for slicing smoked salmon would be useful. A triangular fish knife and fork would be a handy addition.

Carving forks to match and a steel are vital. It may interest students of history to reflect, as they use their carving fork to steady a piece of meat, that until the end of the sixteenth century forks were unheard of in England. Meats were anchored by a smaller knife or skewer and these, with the help of a spoon, did the work of transferring meat slices to platters.

Thereafter, fingers were used for eating. The son of a West Country squire, Tom Coryate, is credited with introducing forks to the British Isles in about 1600, on his return from a Grand Tour of the Continent and a lengthy sojourn in Italy, where forks had been in use for some time. Coryate and his fork were greeted with hoots of derision. He was lampooned on the stage as "the fork-carrying traveler" returned with foreign affectations, and castigated by the clergy, who rose up in pious wrath at the suggestion that "God's good gifts were unfit to be touched by human hands." But times were a-changing. Elizabeth I had introduced a level of feminine daintiness to Court, perpetuated by the Stewarts, and nascent Puritanism was imposing behavioral patterns that extended to the dining room. Stuffing yourself and licking one's fingers no longer had a place at either table. Apart from anything else, the latest fashion in elaborate lace cuffs dictated a change in eating habits.

Early carving forks lacked any form of barrier to stop a knife slipping up the metal bar at the division of the two prongs and straight into the carver's wrist. In response to popular demand, cutlers incorporated small protective hilts into their handle designs, which survived for several hundred years, until the invention of the flange, in the mid-nineteenth century.

So where to find carving knives, forks, and steels? There is an enormous range of high quality chefs' knives made in the latest high technology stainless or carbon steel, but these are essentially kitchen knives. They are perfectly adequate for the job, but not for the dining room if it can be helped. There are still plenty of sets of old Sheffield steel carving knives, still in good condition, to be found in bric-à-brac stores or antique shops around the country, and it is surprising how many are lying about in people's attics. Look for blades at least 1 inch (2.5cm.) in depth that still retain a straight edge and have a handle that firmly fits the blade. There will be plenty of life left in them.

I have a set *circa* 1860 that I use all the time, both at home and at carving demonstrations. Over three days at the Highland Show in 1999, I carved in excess of a hundred pounds of beef and lamb. The soft Sheffield steel blades of these old knives are often discolored, but they can be brought back by rubbing with a paste made from boric acid —ordinary baking soda—and water or vinegar. If you use water, you must put them on blotting paper, after wiping

clean. If using vinegar, simply wipe clean and dry. Wrap in linen or strong paper, never wool which can damage Sheffield steel because it absorbs moisture.

Knives like these were made in the days when they were expected to be in frequent use, and care would have been taken in their balance and the way the horn or polished bone handles fitted the hand. They will be far more pleasant to use than their modern equivalent—rather like the difference between a modern shotgun and a quality London gun made at the turn of the twentieth century. Both will hit, but I would sooner use something made by the old craftsmen.

carving hints

Working on the basis that you are presented with meat that has been properly hung, cooked, and rested, and that your knives are sharp, carving is easy once you have mastered a few simple instructions. Here are one or two basic tips to help you on your way.

● Perhaps the most important is to remember never to apply undue pressure. Let the knife do the work for you and always use the whole length of the blade with long, even strokes. Your aim is for uniform slices which will look appetizing when neatly arranged on the plate. Pressing down will alter the shape of the roast and will lead to uneven slices and a snowball effect through the meat which is almost impossible to correct. Short, jerky sawing at a joint produces uneven, unattractive, jagged slices.

● Keep an eye on the point of your knife to insure that it is in line with the handle to avoid slices that are thicker at one end than the other.

● Nothing is more awkward than trying to carve a small joint or bird with a big knife. Select your knife to suit the size of the roast.

● The edge of your knife is all important. A steel can only maintain the existing edge and it pays to take care of it. When carving on the bone, be sure never to cut down too hard where flesh meets bone, and always use a wooden carving platter when carving rolled, boneless meat. Nothing ruins a good knife as effectively as coming in contact with stainless steel or china.

● If possible, use the fork only to steady meat as you are carving each slice. It is not necessary to plunge it in deeply. This just results in a loss of juices and leaves unsightly puncture holes in the slices.

● Always give yourself lots of room to work in and make sure you have the odd empty plate to remove any detritus to.

● It pays to look after your carving knives and forks, particularly old ones. Do not immerse in soapy water: You will only cause rusting where the shank joins the handle, and it will eventually break. Wipe the blades and fork prongs with a damp cloth. Dry, rub them over with olive oil and pack away safely until they are needed again.

● And, finally, if wearing a tie don't forget to wear a tie clip. Nothing spoils the carver's dignity more than finding the end of his tie floating in the juices...

meat

beef

choosing and cooking beef

The day they finally hang me, I shall have no difficulty in choosing the centerpiece of my last meal. It will be a fore rib —aka a wing rib—of beef. When beef on the bone was about to be banned in the U.K. during the BSE crisis, I bought up every decent fore rib I could get my hands on and stored them in freezers all over East Lothian. I have probably cooked more roasts than most people alive, so I can confidently say I am something of an expert.

When choosing beef I would ask you to throw aside all your preconceived notions. Like almost all meat, beef must be hung to mature, and this is the difference between beef from a good butcher and any other source. The carcass is hung for three to four weeks and loses almost a third of its initial weight, which cost is borne by the butcher and therefore the customer must pay a little more. However, do not begrudge this, for what you lose in the store you gain at the table. Beef properly hung doesn't shrink. How often have you bought your bright red meat, brought it home, cooked it. and discovered to your horror that it has shrunk drastically and will barely serve your guests.

Raw beef when hung should not be bright red; it should be dark, somewhere between garnet-colored and near black. I remember my prudent Edinburgh accountant looking askance at a black piece of fillet his butcher had sold him until he discovered it cooked and ate like a dream. If you are buying a rib, buy it on the bone because meat always cooks sweeter on the bone. It should have a good covering of fat which should be creamy yellow, the shade of homemade clotted cream. Don't get distracted by the cholesterol myth: I am Jack Sprat's wife when it comes to personal choice, and I have the cholesterol levels of a healthy two-year-old child! If your roast has a good layer of fat, you will not need to

baste it and that saves time and effort. It should be marbled —have thin vein-like traceries of fat running through the main joint—like a delicate piece of Carrara stone. Here I do mean delicate and thin; too thick and the beast has been badly fed.

Choose your meat according to your purse. It is better to buy a cheaper cut from a good butcher than a more expensive cut from a cheaper source. If you buy a piece you are pushed to afford, you will worry so much you may very well ruin it. Don't buy cheap filet mignon when sirloin or round steak fits your pocket better, and a good eye of round properly cooked is as heavenly as a rib. It is a rule of thumb that a cheaper cut requires a little more attention and usually a slower cooking to be on equal par, but, hey, once it's in the oven you have more time for a bath, a drink, and even a little *je ne sais quoi*.

roast beef

My mother was determined that anyone who cooked for us should have a foolproof method of roasting beef, so she ruined several good roasts to find the perfect method. It is always better to use a bigger roast than you think you need, as the bigger the roast, the better. If the beef is too lean, ask the butcher to tie some extra fat over the roast. Roasting cuts are rib of beef, sirloin tip, and rolled rump. Calculate the cooking time at 12 minutes per pound (500g.) for very rare, 15 minutes for rare, and 20 for well done on the bone. For a roast off the bone, allow 15, 20, and 25 minutes respectively. A five pound (2.25kg.) roast will serve eight to ten.

Score the fat on the top of theroast and rub it with salt, pepper, and English mustard powder.

Heat the oven to 450°F (230°C).

Place the roast on a rack in a roasting pan and cook 15 minutes (20 if the roast is over 6 pounds/2.75kg.), then turn the heat down to 325°F (160°C). Roast for the remainder of the calculated cooking time.

Remove to a carving dish and allow to rest a final 10 minutes in a warm place. Serve with gravy, horseradish sauce, and Yorkshire pudding (page 149).

no-roast beef

I first heard of this curious method when Johnny's father, Walter, cooked it. Years later I came across it in Robert Carrier's *Cookery Course* and, when I went to my bookstore to look it up, an American customer from Michigan said she always cooked hers this way. It is an excellent way of cooking a roast that is seared without and rare within. However, it will not work with a roast that is less than 5 pounds (2.25kg.) in weight (to serve eight to ten). Some ovens don't hold heat as well as others, so you may want to resort to a thermometer the first time. This cannot be done in an Aga.

Heat your oven to maximum temperature and leave it at least 20 minutes.

Rub the roast with salt and pepper and smear with dripping or butter.

Place the meat on a rack in a roasting pan, put it in the oven, and roast 5 minutes per pound (500g.). Then, turn off the oven without opening it, and leave the meat inside 2 hours.

Open the oven and, without removing the roast, touch it with your fingertips. If it feels hot, serve it. If it feels lukewarm, reheat the oven to maximum temperature and give it a further 10–15 minutes.

spiced beef

This is a traditional Christmas dish in Wales. It is usually made with brisket or bottom round, but you can use skirt or flank which makes it more economical. It is excellent cold for a buffet. You can get hold of saltpeter if you try (my wonderful pharmacist at the Big W at the start of the A1 at Edinburgh got it for me), but if you can't, just leave it out. It's for keeping color really.

Serves 6

2³/4 pounds (1.3kg.) piece of brisket or bottom round
1 cup (200g.) coarse or Kosher salt
1 large onion, finely chopped
1 large carrot, sliced

Spice marinade
1/4 cup (50g.) brown sugar
1/2 teaspoon each ground allspice, cloves, and nutmeg
a pinch each of dried thyme and freshly ground
  black pepper
1 bay leaf, crushed
1 tablespoon saltpeter
2 tablespoons (50g.) molasses, warmed

Bone the beef but don't roll it, then rub it thoroughly on all sides with salt and leave overnight. Drain the beef from the salt and wipe dry.

For the marinade, mix the sugar, allspice, cloves, nutmeg, thyme, pepper, bay, and saltpeter together. Rub the beef on both sides with the spices and leave covered in a cool place two days (the salad crisper of the refrigerator will do). Pour the warmed molasses over the meat and rub with the spices every day for a week.

Roll the beef up firmly and tie with string. Put in a pan of boiling water with the onion and carrot. Bring to a boil, skim, and simmer gently, covered, 3 hours. Leave to cool in the liquid, then remove.

Place the meat on a flat board, and put another board on top of it. Press with a heavy weight about 24 hours in the refrigerator before serving.

beef will moreland

This recipe, designed for top round, was given to me by a young man I once worked with who is as talented a violinist and artist as he is a cook. Being of an extravagant disposition, I adapted it for sirloin. It is a recipe I have cooked many times in many places: it has always found favour and never let me down. Thank you, Will.

Serves 4

2¼ pounds (1kg.) boneless beef (sirloin tip or rolled rump)
2 tablespoons vegetable oil
2 garlic cloves, chopped
a thumb-sized piece of fresh ginger, chopped
a bunch of scallions, chopped
1 tablespoon soy sauce
a large bunch of cilantro, chopped
2 fresh chilies, chopped
1 piece of lemongrass, chopped
2 cans coconut milk
juice of 1 lime

Heat the oven to 350°F (180°C). Heat a heavy skillet and seal your meat, then remove it. Heat the oil in the same pan and sauté the garlic, ginger, and scallions until softened. Add the soy sauce, half the cilantro, and the chilies. (The heat of the chilies is a matter of choice: use a Scotch bonnet for ultra hot or a jalapeño for mild.) Place the meat in a roasting pan and surround with the fried vegetable mixture. Add the lemongrass and pour over the coconut milk and lime juice. Cook in the oven 40 minutes. Transfer the beef to a serving dish. Add the rest of the cilantro to the juices, pour over the meat, and serve immediately. For a fancy sauce you can strain and reduce it, but I don't.

royal brisket

This recipe is from John Farley's *The London Art of Cookery*, published in 1783, and it is delicious. Oysters and beef were a common combination at this time and go very well together, but if you balk at the oysters use anchovies.

Serves 4

2¼ pounds (1kg.) piece of boneless brisket
¼ pound (100g.) bacon, chopped
4 oysters, shucked and chopped
2 tablespoons chopped parsley
salt and freshly ground black pepper
freshly grated nutmeg
⅓ cup (50g.) all-purpose flour
½ stick (50g.) butter
2½ cups (600ml.) red wine
⅔ cup (150ml.) brown stock

Make incisions all over the meat 1 inch (2.5cm.) apart. Stuff the slits alternately with bacon, oyster, and parsley. Season with salt, pepper, and nutmeg, then dredge with flour.

Heat the butter in a skillet and brown the meat all over. Place in a large flameproof casserole with the wine and stock, and bring slowly to a boil. Cover tightly, reduce to a gentle simmer, and cook gently on top of the stove 3 hours. Serve with the skimmed juices.

mexican brisket

This is a Mexican recipe from my friend Lydia Garcia, to whom I owe a debt of gratitude. She lives in Chihuahua, the ancient capital, where ancho chilies are much used. They are not very hot, and when dried they have a wonderful smoky flavor. They can be bought in good gourmet stores or ordered by mail. Check the Internet for sources.

Serves 6

2³/₄ pounds (1.3kg.) piece of brisket
¹/₄ pound (125g.) bacon, diced
1¹/₂ tablespoons slivered almonds
3 tablespoons lard or bacon fat
1¹/₂ pounds (700g.) new potatoes, parboiled for 5 minutes
  and peeled

Chili paste
3 large ancho chilies
3 cloves
¹/₃ inch (1cm.) cinnamon stick
a pinch each of dried thyme, marjoram. and oregano
6 black peppercorns
2 garlic cloves, peeled
2 teaspoons salt
2 tablespoons red wine vinegar
1 cup (225ml.) water

Make incisions in the beef and insert the diced bacon and almond slivers.

For the chili paste, toast the chilies in a heavy pan, then slit them open, and remove the seeds and veins. Put the chilies in a bowl of hot water and soak 20 minutes. Drain and put them in a blender, add all the remaining chili paste ingredients, and reduce to a paste.

Preheat the oven to 325°F (160°C).

Heat the lard or bacon fat in a flameproof casserole and brown the meat all over. Remove the meat, and drain off all the fat. Return 3 tablespoons of fat to the pan and add the chlli mixture. Cook, stirring constantly, 5 minutes over a brisk heat.

Return the meat to the casserole and spoon the chili mixture over it. Cover tightly and cook in the oven 2 hours. Turn the meat, baste, and arrange the potatoes around the meat. Scrape the sides of the casserole and add a little water if the sauce is too thick. Cook a further 1 hour and 10 minutes, and serve with the potatoes and sauce.

beef wellington

This dish has nothing to do with that splendid hero, the Duke of Wellington; it was invented for a civic reception in Wellington, New Zealand, but it is a splendid addition to any party. The idea of cooking something in a pastry "coffin" dates back to the Middle Ages and, unlike a pie, a coffin was not intended to be eaten. The French *filet de boeuf en croûte* uses either sausagemeat or mushrooms; Beef Wellington differs in that you use a coarse pâté. I use readymade puff pastry, but I will give you the entire recipe here, using a short piecrust dough.

Serves 6

2³/4 pounds (1.3kg.) tenderloin roast or sirloin tip
2 ounces (50g.) coarse game pâté
1 teaspoon salt

Pastry
3¹/2 cups (450g.) all-purpose flour, sifted
1 stick + 2 tablespoons (140g.) softened butter, diced
3 eggs
3 tablespoons vegetable oil

For the pastry, sift the flour into a mound on your work surface, and make a well in the center. Put the butter, 2 whole eggs, and the third egg white and the oil in the center, and work to a dough. Roll into a ball, place in plastic wrap, and refrigerate a day. If you are desperate, 2 hours will do.

Preheat the oven to 400°F (200°C).

Seal the meat on a hot fatless skillet until browned all over, and leave to cool.

Roll out the pastry on a floured board into a rectangle and spread a central oblong with the pâté. Season the meat with salt, then put it in the centre of the dough. Wrap the dough around the meat and seal the edges with water. Place on a baking sheet, join downward. Paint the pastry with the remaining egg yolk mixed with a little water.

Cook in the oven about 50 minutes until the pastry is golden brown. Cover with foil if pastry is browning too much.

boiled beef and dumplings

Real comfort food on a cold winter's day. I save chicken fat to make my dumplings in the Jewish way: The traditional fat is beef suet, but you can use lard or butter (chill these, then coarsely grate). I cheat and use self-rising flour, but purists will use all-purpose flour and add the soda. (If you get it wrong, it will do for shot-putting!) The horseradish makes a good sharp accompaniment to the beef.

Serves 6

2³/4 pounds (1.3kg.) boneless brisket or rump, rolled
  and tied
1 small knuckle of veal
1 tablespoon salt
1 large onion, halved
4 carrots, sliced
3 leeks, sliced
1/2 head celery, chopped
1 bay leaf

Herb and horseradish dumplings
3/4 cup (100g.) self-rising flour
1²/3 cups (100g.) fresh white breadcrumbs
2 ounces (50g.) fat (see above)
2 tablespoons mixed fresh herbs (whatever's about, but
  thyme, marjoram, chervil, parsley *et al*)
1/3 cup (40g.) grated horseradish
salt and freshly ground black pepper
2 eggs, beaten

Place the beef and the knuckle of veal in a large flameproof Dutch oven or casserole, cover with cold water, and bring slowly to a boil, skimming carefully and often. Add the salt after 10 minutes. Half cover and simmer 2 hours. Carefully spoon off any fat from the top of the liquid. Add the vegetables and bay leaf and simmer another hour, adding the dumplings 30 minutes before the end of cooking.

To make the dumplings, mix the flour with all the other ingredients except the eggs, then stir in the beaten eggs to form a soft dough. Shape into eight large or sixteen small balls. Add to the boiling beef 30 minutes before the end of cooking.

rhineland sauerbraten

This dish, variants of which are found all over Germany, was given to my mother by a German friend who used to come to help us with our swinefests in the days when my father kept pigs. The difference lies in the gravy, which is thickened with Lebkuchen (Christmas gingerbread biscuits) crumbs, apple syrup, and raisins. All these are obtainable at a good German grocery or on the Internet, but if in doubt use gingerbread crumbs and molasses. Venison is also good done like this.

Serves 4–6

2¼–2¾ pounds (1–1.3kg.) boneless sirloin or rump,
  rolled and tied
⅓ cup (75g.) lard
½ cup (100g.) raisins, soaked in a little water
salt and freshly ground black pepper
⅔ cup (75g.) Lebkuchen crumbs
1 tablespoon apple syrup
1 cup (225ml.) sour cream

Marinade
2½ cups (600ml.) water
1¼ cups (300ml.) white wine vinegar
1 teaspoon salt
2 onions, halved
1 carrot, sliced
a handful of black peppercorns
2 bay leaves
6 cloves

For the marinade, put all the ingredients in a large pan, bring to a boil, and simmer 20 minutes. Set aside to cool. Place the meat in the cool marinade and leave 2–3 days in a cool place, turning occasionally.

Heat the oven to 350°F (180°C).

After marinating, dry the beef with a cloth, then heat the lard in a skillet and brown the beef all over to seal. Drain the marinade, discarding the vegetables, and pour the liquid back over the meat in a large casserole or Dutch oven. Roast in the oven 1½ hours, basting from time to time. About 15 minutes before the end of the cooking time, add the drained raisins. Transfer the cooked meat to a dish.

Deglaze the casserole, season the sauce with salt and pepper, and thicken with the crumbs. Stir in the syrup and sour cream. Serve with potato pancakes.

chateaubriand

This magnificent dish, called after a great statesman, uses the whole of the center tenderloin, about 1 pound (500g.) in weight. It is traditionally served very rare with a sauce made of meat jelly, to which twice its weight of *maître d'hotel* butter is added, and sautéed potatoes. My brother and I once sent one back at Rules restaurant because it was overcooked, and you'd have thought we'd assassinated the chef. The meat must be larded with beef fat or wrapped in strips of fat because it is so dry that roasting without this will render it inedible.

Serves 2–3

1 porterhouse steak, about 1 pound (400–500g.)
chilled beef fat, cut into long thin strips
salt and freshly ground black pepper

Sauce
1 stick (100g.) butter
1 tablespoon chopped parsley
1 teaspoon lemon juice
2 tablespoons reduced meat stock, set to a jelly

Heat the oven to 400°F (200°C).

Using a larding needle or a thin sharp knife, lard the steak with the strips of fat, and season with pepper.

Lay the meat on a baking tray and roast it in the oven, seasoning with salt halfway through cooking. The timing is a matter of choice: I like my meat very rare and cook it 15 minutes only, but between 20 and 30 minutes is more usual.

For the sauce, mix the butter with the parsley and lemon juice, and season with salt and pepper. Heat the jellied stock gently and add the butter in small pieces, mixing well to emulsify and thicken.

carving beef

sirloin

Right, the great moment has come. In front of us on the sideboard a beautiful standing sirloin rib roast sits on a serving dish, filling the room with the exquisite aroma of roast beef. The word "sirloin" is a corruption of the French *surloin*, meaning "above the loin," and should correctly be spelled with "u." What is, in fact, no more than a spelling mistake has been romanticized by devotees of this particular cut with the story that a loin of beef was raised to the knighthood by a monarch. According to tradition, James I, a noted trencherman, was staying with Sir Richard Hoghton at Hoghton Tower near Blackburn in 1617. Going in to dinner, King James spotted a mighty loin of beef and, in a "frolic," drew out his sword and knighted it.

Our novice carver nonchalantly strokes the blade of his knife on the steel, his kneecaps jerking with anxiety. Before him is about one hundred bucks worth of meat, behind him a smart dinner party of eight. There is no going back, my son, so carry on. The sirloin should be standing with the chine bone—that is, the remaining half of the backbone—vertical and the meat and ribs facing you.

Insert your fork in the middle of the meat and toward the top. At the top of the prongs a carving fork has a flange, which should be lifted. Its purpose is to stop the blade sinking into the wrist. Nothing is guaranteed to ruin a party quicker than the carver being rushed to the hospital and, although he will have no reason to carve toward the body on this occasion, it is one less thing to worry about.

Grip the carving fork in the left hand and cut down to the rib next to the chine bone between the meat. Next, trim off any gristle and tough sinuous tissues at the top where the meat has been joined to the chine bone. These will prevent the smooth entry of the knife and so it is important to remove them.

You now need to make an incision from the end of the meat down the length and depth of the first rib, so the first few slices fall free as you carve them. A 10 pound (4.5kg.) roast is small enough to lift, so turn the roast on its side to do this. Now, making sure that your knife is in line with the ribs, make an incision $1/8$ inch (3mm.) in from the end. This is the optimum width to maximize the delicious flavor of roast beef. Smaller than this and you miss it; larger—and Americans go for twice the size—and you may as well have a steak in the first place. Cut boldly downward, and, as the slice falls free, lift it with the knife blade onto a plate.

Remember, do not press down. Your knife is sharp: Let it do the work for you (see page 22). Your aim is for even slices that will look appetizing when neatly arranged on the plate.

As you continue carving, making your incision along the rib bones as you go, angle your cuts very slightly at the top to avoid undercutting.

1 Make an initial 2 inch (5cm.) cut between meat and top bone (if present).

2 Slice at corresponding depth between meat and rib bone.

3 Carve slices $^{1}/_{8}$ inch (3mm.) wide.

4 This is a wing rib without the sirloin, but for a sirloin turn over and carve generous slices of fillet.

1 The fore rib.

2 Remove the top flap by cutting around the rib eye.

fore rib/wing rib: 1

Once you have successfully carved a sirloin to great acclaim and been the wonder and envy of your guests, the next challenge is the fore rib. Of the twelve ribs of a side of beef, in the U.K. the first eight are called "the undercut" and the "wing-rib" sirloin. Next to them, and running into the shoulder, is the "fore rib." If a cup of Ovaltine is synonymous with Britain in the 1950s, this cut, for all the government's limitations on size, invokes the atmosphere of Regency England, conjuring up visions of low-beamed coaching inns, boozy hunt dinners and, nowadays, the most splendid luncheon parties. If my children didn't insist on turkey at Christmas, it would make a truly magnificent alternative.

Because we are moving towards the massive locomotive machinery of the beast, the fore rib has a greater fat covering and necessitates a large roast, not less than 10 pounds (4.5kg.), to do it justice and stretch the carver's ability. Last Christmas I shared in a stunning 20-pounder (9kg.)—combining wing rib and fore rib—an awesome sight.

For a sizeable fore rib, make sure you have lots of room to maneuver in and an extra wooden serving platter. The best meat of a fore rib, the ribeye, is protected by a thick layer of delicious fat through which runs a strip of toughish meat. This can make the fluidity of carving awkward, and should be removed in its entirety.

Loosen the top flap by cutting along the top bone and down, but not into, the ribeye. Now, insert the carving fork into the top flap at the right-hand edge of the rib roast and cut around the ribeye down to the end of the ribs, twisting the fork upward so the top flap lifts away. You will be slicing through a layer of subcutaneous fat which the knife will bisect easily as you proceed along the length of the ribeye. The top flap comes away smoothly and, once free, should be placed on the separate platter and a slice of the golden fat added to each plate. The well-cooked meat of the top flap can be served to children not yet old enough to appreciate rare meat.

With the top flap off, the carver is confronted with a piece pretty similar to a sirloin. The meat will have more marbling and strands of fat running through it, and be less compact than a sirloin. Because the meat is not so firm, greater care is required to avoid bulging which will give you an uneven slice, and maintaining the edge of your blade is important. As with any roast, always remember to angle your knife very slightly towards your fork. Otherwise, the same principles apply. Slices should be 1/8 inch (3mm.) thick.

Cut along the space between the bone and the meat and between the meat and the ribs, every few slices. Add a piece of fat and a spoonful of juices to the meat on each plate and, above all, enjoy yourself. This is a festive occasion and it's not every day you have the opportunity to step back in time.

For the wing rib, see pictures on page 31.

Smaller fore rib roasts

Because of its position on the animal, and the higher fat content, a fore rib is by far the most flavorsome, juicy, and succulent of all the beef roast cuts. The meat is much less firm than the neighboring sirloin, and therefore a larger roast is more practical and easier to manage for the carver. For this reason, a sizeable piece is generally bought. Smaller pieces of only two ribs are often overlooked, which is a pity, because they make a delicious entrée at a small party. What puts people off them, the perceived difficulty in carving a fore rib roast of this size, is surmounted by simply using a different technique and carving parallel to the top bone (if there is one), rather than at right angles to it.

Turn the roast so the top bone is at right angles to your body and in line with your carving arm. Removing the top flap as before, trim off any gristle at the top of the bone and cut down to the ribs between the meat and the bone. With the next slice, 1/8 inch (3mm.) thick, when the knife reaches the bone, angle it slightly and cut towards the top bone to free the slice. Continue cutting slices down the length of the ribs, angling the knife to free each slice as you go.

3 Slice the eye fillet. To maximize flavor, slices must be
¹/₈ inch (3mm.) thick.

4 Cut along the top bone between the bone and meat
every few slices.

beef off the bone

For beef off the bone the principles of carving are pretty much the same as for a loaf of bread and about as interesting. Sirloin tip, rolled rump, brisket, and, of course, tenderloin are generally carved off the bone, for the very good reason that the bone structures to which they are attached scarcely lend themselves to the dining-room sideboard. Why anyone should want to take either of the sirloins or the fore rib off the bone is beyond me and is, I suspect, directly connected to the lack of knowledge of how to carve. But there we are. We live in strange times, and if confronted by one of these insults to good beef, must carry our cross with as much dignity as possible.

A whole tenderloin should be carved across the grain in generous 1/4 inch (5mm.) slices. Rump, boiled brisket, and all other boneless cuts should be carved in the usual 1 inch (3mm.) thickness. Roasts that have been taken off the bone, rolled, and tied with string—the sirloins, brisket, and fore ribs—can be carved in two different ways.

For a small roast, say 2 1/4–2 3/4 pounds (2.25–2.75kg.), the carver has more control over the roast if it is placed with the round bottom surface flat on the server and the meat carved across the top. You will be relying on your fork to keep the meat steady. Insert it at an angle of 30 degrees, 1/2 inch (1cm.) from the top. Make sure the knife is absolutely level with the top of the roast and make the first incision, slicing towards the fork. This is where the flange comes into its own. A certain amount of concentration is required, checking that the blade remains level as it moves across the roast. It would be a pity, halfway through the operation, to become distracted by the thought that it was heading inexorably towards an unprotected forearm.

Larger joints can be carved initially, lying on their side, held in place by the fork inserted in the top, moving it back as carving progresses. Slices are carved straight down towards the serving platter, taking care that the knife is angled very slightly to avoid undercutting. Remember that there is no bone to protect the edge of your knife, so try to make sure that the carving board is wooden (nothing blunts a knife more quickly than china or steel). When a third of the roast is left, or at the point it begins to become wobbly, turn it so the bottom faces downward and reposition the fork. At this stage the roast will undoubtedly need some trimming and leveling before the carver is able to continue cutting even slices. This is the moment when the family dog, drooling in anticipation, should be rewarded for its patience. The last few slices before the roast is finished are always a little tricky because the meat is now losing all rigidity. Hopefully no more meat will be required, but in the event that some is needed it will probably be necessary to turn the fork on its side with only one prong inserted in the meat and the upper acting in place of the flange.

beef cuts

Give them great meals of beef and iron and steel,
They will eat like wolves and fight like devils.

Shakespeare

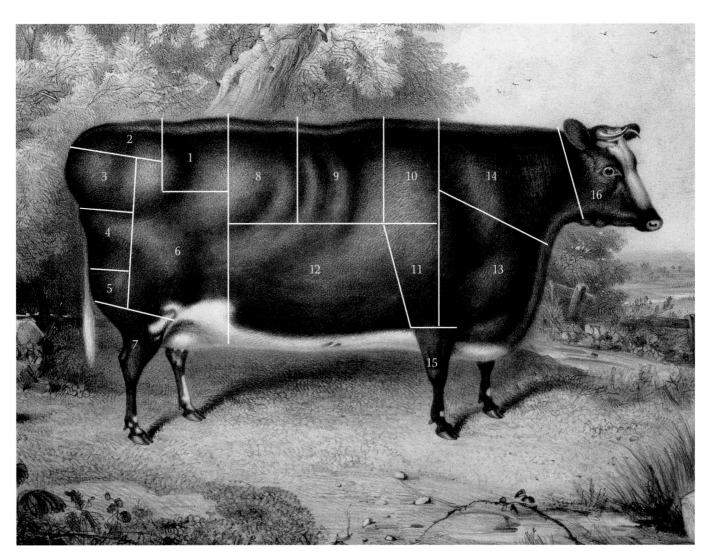

1 Sirloin (sirloin)

2 Rump (round)

3 Top side (top round)

4 Thick flank (bottom round)

5 Thick flank (eye round)

6 Flank and suet (bottom sirloin and short loin)

7 Shin (shank)

8 Wing rib (ribeye)

9 Fore rib (rib)

10 Chuck (chuck)

11 Shank (bottom sirloin)

12 Rolled ribs and brisket (flank and brisket)

13 Shank (brisket)

14 Neck (chuck)

15 Shin (shank)

16 Cheek (cheek)

lamb and mutton

choosing and cooking lamb and mutton

Lamb is the young of the sheep family; it is young until it is one-year-old when it becomes hogget in the U.K. but mutton in the U.S.A. Only after two years does it become mutton in the U.K. Milk lamb or suckling lamb is seldom sold in Britain or the U.S.A, but is popular in France, Italy, and Spain. It is very tender and the cuts are very small. Spring lamb is the small lean cuts of lamb specially brought on for Easter, and new season's lamb, which comes after Easter, is still lean with small joints. As the year goes by the lambs are weaned from their mothers and fattened. Most lambs are taken and fattened as store lambs on turnips and grain, and taste rather muddy. To choose lamb insure that the fat is a good color—like very rich or clotted cream—and the meat a clear dark pink.

Mutton is eaten less now in Britain, although it was the pride of the country when it was a wool-raising nation, four-year-old black-faced mutton being best of all. There, it is mostly eaten by the West Indian and Pakistani communities who know a good thing when they see it, and can often be found curried. It has a strong distinctive taste, but I do recommend it to you. It may be very difficult to track down in the U.S.A, but try it and you may be delighted. Try to avoid hogget, identifiable by its large joints and darker-coloured flesh. One-year-old lamb falls between both stools and is better used as stewing meat. The most usual roasting cuts are leg and shoulder, but I have rung all the changes for you from a splendid saddle to fine hindquarters. I have also given you the cheaper cut of collar which is the neck and breast of lamb. It is said that people don't like the taste of lamb. Well, neither do I when it is fattened on turnips, but good lamb is beyond compare.

roast leg of lamb

The classic way of cooking this is to make incisions all over the roast and put slivers of garlic and rosemary into the holes prior to cooking. There are many variants on this theme, including anchovies or fresh ginger—use your own imagination. The recipe I have chosen to give is an unusual one from Bert Greene who has adapted the North African method of using pickled lemons. It is very good, but requires a bit more effort. Allow 10–12 minutes per pound (500g.) for rare, 15 minutes for medium-rare, 20 minutes for well done.

Serves 6–8

1 leg of lamb, about 6 pounds (2.75kg)
2 lemons
1–2 large garlic cloves, slivered
1 tablespoon Dijon mustard
1/2 teaspoon ground ginger
2 tablespoons olive oil
salt and freshly ground black pepper

Peel the lemons, keeping the zest in one long strip. Cut each strip into three so that you have six long strips.

Without breaking the skin, score the surface of the lamb with cross-hatched diagonal lines at 1½ inch (4cm.) intervals. Thread one long strip of zest into the eye of a larding needle. Make small holes every inch (2.5cm.) along these score marks, using the larding needle. Weave the lemon strips along the holes in the score marks, going in at one, under the skin, and out at another—just as if darning a sock. The finished surface of the lamb should resemble a woven basket.

Make several small incisions between the lemon zests and insert slivers of garlic. Place the roast in a roasting pan. Squeeze the lemons and combine the juice with the rest of the ingredients. Spoon over the lamb and refrigerate for 2 hours.

Heat the oven to 450°F (230°C).

Roast the lamb in the oven 15 minutes. Reduce the heat to 325°F (160°C). Baste every 15 minutes and cook the remaining calculated cooking time. Rest 10 minutes before carving.

roast saddle of lamb

A saddle of lamb looks dramatic and yields plenty of meat, provided you know how to carve it. Now, thanks to Johnny, you will! It is not particularly difficult to cook, but be careful not to let it dry out as there is a lot of bone.

Serves 6

1 saddle of lamb, about 2³/₄–3¹/₃ pounds (1.3–1.5kg.)
4 tablespoons olive oil
3 garlic cloves
1 teaspoon dried thyme
salt and freshly ground black pepper
5 tablespoons water or dry white wine

Calculate the cooking time at 25 minutes per pound (500g.).

Heat the oven to 425°F (220°C).

Trim the fat right down over the roast, although this is not usually necessary in today's meat, which is overlean. Rub the whole roast well with the oil and garlic, and sprinkle the thyme on the top side. Rub the underside of the roast with salt and pepper and fold the apron under the roast until the two rolls touch. Secure with string or a skewer. Place in a close-fitting, heavy roasting pann, then into the oven 10 minutes only.

Reduce the heat to 325°F (160°C) for the remainder of the calculated cooking time. As you turn the oven down, season the top of the meat and pour in the water or wine. Baste the roast with the pan juices twice during the cooking time. Remove the joint from the oven and allow to rest at least 10 minutes before carving.

rack of lamb with garlic

I was very surprised when I discovered that my favorite nun, Mer April O'Leary, a woman of infinite culinary skill and variety who now lives in a small community, had never heard of this cut which is so perfect for two people. It is totally easy to cook and carve, and is a truly delicious treat, especially if the lamb comes from the little black-faced sheep that Johnny loves so much.

Serves 4

2 racks of lamb, about 8 cutlets each
salt and freshly ground black pepper
2 teaspoons cumin seeds
2 garlic bulbs, cloves separated but unpeeled

Heat the oven to 425°F (220°C).

Season the skin of the meat with salt and pepper and sprinkle the seeds over the two racks. Place on a wire rack in a roasting pan and put the garlic cloves around the lamb.

Roast in the oven between 45 and 55 minutes, depending on how you like your lamb. Serve with the garlic cloves, which squeeze out into a soft paste. If you want to be tidy, squeeze them into a pan and stir in a little butter and seasoning.

hindquarter of lamb with herbs

roast shoulder of lamb

This unusual cut makes a wonderful party dish. You should allow 9–18 minutes per pound (500g.) depending on how you like your lamb. I usually allow 12 minutes per pound (500g.).

Serves 12–16

1 hindquarter of lamb
1/2 pound (250g.) sliced bacon
1/2 cup (75g.) dried breadcrumbs
2 1/4 cups (500ml.) white wine or stock
5 shallots, chopped
2/3 cup (150ml.) orange and lemon juices mixed

Stuffing
1/2 pound (250g.) bacon, rind removed, and finely chopped
1 stick (100g.) soft butter
1/4 pound (125g.) mushrooms, chopped
6 scallions, chopped
2 garlic cloves, finely chopped
1 3/4 cups (50g.) parsley, chopped
2 tablespoons chopped herbs (parsley, chervil, tarragon)
1 tablespoon mixed spice

Heat the oven to 450°F (230°C). Loosen the skin on the lamb without tearing. Mix all the stuffing ingredients together, and ease the mixture between the skin and flesh of the lamb. Wrap the lamb in the bacon and then in foil. Cook the lamb in the oven 10 minutes to seal it, then reduce the heat to 350°F (180°C) for the remaining calculated cooking time. About 15 minutes before the end, remove the foil and bacon. Sprinkle with the breadcrumbs and brown slightly. Transfer to a serving dish to rest. Deglaze the pan with the wine or stock, then add the shallots, and stir over a high heat until the sauce is reduced by one third. Stir in the orange and lemon juices, and serve the gravy with the lamb.

The shoulder is known as the butcher's cut because it is the one most favored by the trade for their own consumption. It is a very versatile cut, suitable for straight roasting on a rack (since it can be fatty), for cooking in a casserole (as is most commonly done in Greece, a great nation for lamb), for stuffing, or for barbecuing (when it would be butterflied— that is, split). An average shoulder will serve four to six.

To roast, simply incise the joint with garlic and herbs and roast in an oven heated to 350°F (180°C) 15 minutes per pound (500g.).

boiled mutton

Leg, shoulder, neck, and flank are all suitable for this recipe. It is a wonderful dish and delicious with caper or onion sauce. Cucumber cream sauce, apple sauce, and even dill sauce are found in historical records as accompaniments. If the mutton is fatty, trim it back. Allow 20 minutes per pound (500g.) plus an extra 25 minutes.

Allow about 1/2 pound (225g.) meat per person.

1 piece of mutton
sweet fresh herbs tied together (thyme, marjoram,
  parsley, chervil)
1 onion, stuck with cloves
2 teaspoons salt
1/2 pound (250g.) each carrots and turnips,
  coarsely chopped

Put the meat in a large pan and cover with boiling water. Add the herbs and onion, bring to a boil, and skim well. Boil 5 minutes, then reduce to a simmer. Halfway through the cooking time, add the salt. About 30 minutes before the end of the cooking time add the carrots and turnips.

Serve the mutton with the vegetables. The broth, when cooled and skimmed, makes a wonderful basis for onion soup.

spiced mutton

A medieval dish traditionally served with red currant jelly and a salad of sharp greens. The mutton used was probably salted. The cut you choose is dependent on your pocket, but leg is probably the most likely. Allow 30 minutes per pound (500g.).

A 5 pound (2.25kg.) leg will serve eight to ten.

1 piece of mutton
3/4 cup (75g.) fine oatmeal
1/2 teaspoon each ground thyme, ground black pepper,
  and mace
oil or dripping
cabbage leaves
2/3 cup (150ml.) hard cider or apple juice
2/3 cup (150ml.) red wine

Heat the oven to 350°F (180°C).

Mix together the oatmeal, thyme, pepper, and mace. Rub the meat with oil or add dabs of dripping, then coat with the spiced oatmeal, and wrap in cabbage leaves to keep in the spices and prevent the meat from browning.

Roast the mutton in the oven, basting with the cider or apple juice. About 40 minutes before the end of the cooking time, pour off the surplus fat and remove the cabbage leaves. Pour over the red wine and baste during the remaining cooking time. Serve with the pan juices.

stuffed shoulder
with eggplant

This is a Greek recipe. In Greece they usually roast the shoulder and cut the leg into collops, recognizing what a lovely, sweet-tasting cut the shoulder is. To make it go further, it is quite usual to stuff it, and you can of course use anything your heart desires. To get you started, this uses eggplant.

Serves 6–8

4¹/₂ pounds (2kg.) shoulder of lamb, boned
salt and freshly ground black pepper
1 pound (500g.) eggplant, peeled and thinly sliced
about ²/₃ cup (175ml.) olive oil
1 onion, grated
1 garlic clove, crushed
1 tablespoon each chopped mint and parsley
2 tablespoons chopped oregano
1 cup (225ml.) white wine
juice of ¹/₂ lemon
4 small baking potatoes, halved and parboiled
** 5 minutes**
sprigs of fresh herbs to garnish

Heat the oven to 450°F (230°C).

Season the eggplant slices and brown them on both sides in half of the olive oil (you may need more) until almost cooked. Remove and drain very well. Add a little more oil to the pan and brown the onion and garlic, then add the chopped mint and parsley and half the chopped oregano. Lay the shoulder flat and spread the onion mixture over the inside of the lamb. Season and put the eggplant slices on top. Roll and tie the lamb, put in a roasting pan, and pour over half the wine.

Roast the lamb in the oven 15 minutes to brown it, then reduce the heat to 300°F (150°C) and roast 1¹/₂ hours for pink lamb, 2¹/₂ hours for well done. Combine the remaining oil with the lemon juice and use this to baste the lamb frequently.

About 30 minutes before the lamb is cooked, put the potatoes in the pan around the meat, season them, and sprinkle with the remaining chopped oregano. When the lamb is cooked, remove it and the potatoes to a serving dish. Skim the juices, add the remaining wine, adjust the seasoning, and simmer several minutes. Serve this gravy with the lamb. Garnish with the fresh herb sprigs.

spit-roasted lamb

crown roast or guard of honour

I have included this recipe because I have frequently been asked for it over the last fifteen years. An alternative method, highly attractive but frankly unlikely nowadays, is to find a friendly baker with an old-fashioned oven who will half-cook it for you as his oven cools.

Serves 50+

1 lamb, about 50 pounds (22.5kg.) in weight
juice of 2 lemons (keep the zest)
salt and freshly ground black pepper
a few large sprigs of thyme
a few large sprigs of oregano or rosemary
1¹/₂ cups (350ml.) olive oil
3–4 garlic cloves, crushed

Wipe the lamb inside and out with a damp cloth. Rub the inside of the beast with the lemon halves and season with salt and pepper. Put half the herbs into the cavity and close it with skewers. Set the lamb on its stomach and push the spit through the center, through the anus, along the back of the spine, and through the neck. Pull the forelegs forward and tie them securely to the spit with wire. Put the back legs along the spit, cross them, and secure with wire.

Mix the lemon juice, olive oil, garlic, and some salt and pepper. Wrap the remaining herbs in muslin and soak in the oil mixture. Start the fire in a pit or a large metal drum and let it burn until the flames die down. Add a layer of charcoal and put the spitted lamb on the stands. To begin, keep it well above the fire and turn slowly. Lower nearer the fire halfway through the cooking. Baste with the oil, using the herb sprigs. Cook 6–7 hours over the coals, adding more charcoal as needed.

Two dishes to get your butcher to prepare for you. With Guard of Honour you can stuff the cavity after cooking with mushrooms or small potatoes cooked separately. With the Crown Roast, it is stuffed before cooking.

Serves 4–6

2 lamb loins, with rib bones attached
salt and freshly ground black pepper
chopped fresh thyme or rosemary

Heat the oven to 375°F (190°C) .

Turn the lamb racks skin side up and remove 1 inch (3cm.) of skin and fat from the end of the bones (this is known as"frenching"). Score the skin in diamonds. Rub the salt, pepper, and herbs into the skin.

For the Guard of Honour, stand the racks skin side out and push together so the bones cross alternately. Skewer the meat at the base, protect exposed bones with foil, and roast in the oven 1¹/₂ hours.

For the Crown Roast, the racks are curved and tied into a circle, fat side in. The "cavity" is filled with a stiff herb, breadcrumb, and forcemeat stuffing bound with egg—or use the Apricot and Apple Stuffing on page 152—and roasted in the same manner as above.

breton leg of lamb

When I used to go regularly to Brittany to eat oysters, I would take great delight in this traditional dish made with dried white beans. It is another great comfort dish.

Serves 6

1 leg of lamb, about 4^1/$_2$ pounds (2kg.)
^{3}/$_4$ stick (75g.) butter

Beans
2^1/$_2$ cups (500g.) dried white beans, such as kidney beans
1 carrot
1 onion, stuck with a clove
1 bouquet garni (thyme, bay leaf, and parsley)
salt and freshly ground black pepper
^{1}/$_4$ pound (175g.) lean smoked ham (in a piece)
1^1/$_4$ cups (300ml.) heavy cream
^{3}/$_4$ stick (75g.) butter
soft white breadcrumbs

Soak the beans in lots of water overnight. Drain and place in a pan of cold water, then add the carrot, onion, and bouquet garni. Bring to a boil, cover, and cook until tender, about 50 minutes. Drain, remove the vegetables, and season with salt and pepper. Set aside. Heat the oven to 350°F (180°C). Spread the lamb with the butter and roast in the oven 12 minutes per pound (500g.). Season halfway through. About 25 minutes before the meat is ready, finish the beans. Cube the ham and brown in a hot pan. Add to the beans along with the cream and most of the butter. Place in a baking dish, cover with breadcrumbs, and dot with the remaining butter. Bake for 30 minutes alongside the lamb. Serve the roast with the beans and its own juices in a separate dish.

butterflied leg of lamb

This is a cut wherein the lamb is split open and flattened with most of the bone removed to cook more quickly on a barbecue.

Serves 6

1 leg of lamb, butterflied

Baste
1 large pot tapenade (you can make your own but I don't for this dish)
2 garlic cloves, finely chopped
1 small can anchovies
^{1}/$_2$ cup (125ml.) olive oil
juice of 2 lemons
1 tablespoon chopped fresh oregano or marjoram

Mix all the baste ingredients together and spread liberally on all sides of the lamb. Cook, initially over a hot flame on the barbecue to seal the meat, turning frequently for about 15–20 minutes, then remove the meat further from the coals and cook another 1^1/$_2$ hours, basting with more of the mixture plus a little extra oil.

carving lamb and mutton

leg of lamb

"Of the sheep is cast away nothing" is the opening verse of a thirteenth-century couplet which then goes to eulogize parts of the animal most modern housewives wouldn't dream of touching, or which have been banned by the government. Sheep's head broth is known to us only from history books. Brawn? Mutton pies? Lambs' tail pie? Mutton hams or sausages? Boiled salt mutton and caper sauce? All things of the past and all there to be brought back to life again as eating standards and food quality improve.

A decent sized roast leg of wether lamb off a beast that has been naturally grown on the land it was born on— in the U.K. the springy turf of the South Downs or the gentle heather hills of southern Scotland—is a deliciousroast and as different from the mediocre meat of a turnip-finished lamb as chalk from cheese.

One great advantage of a leg of lamb is the bone protruding from the knuckle end with which the carver can take a firm grip. If you really want to be flash, the bone can be covered with a paper frill. If you simply want to get on with the job, a small clean cloth will do.

Taking hold of the bone, turn the leg so that the area of thickest meat, the back of the thigh, is uppermost.

Open the roast by cutting a narrow wedge of meat out at the point where the knuckle end begins to widen. Remove and set aside. Now you can get in at the joint. Lamb and mutton have a slightly elusive flavor and slices need to be a little thicker than beef.

Carve slices down to and over the bone, angling the knife towards the knuckle end as you reach the bone, to free each slice. Proceed as far as the pelvic bone will allow.

Then turn the leg and carve the remainder of the meat on the thin side, parallel to the bone.

Remember that you have no fork and protecting flange, so "gaw canny."

a leg of mutton or large leg of lamb

In the days when wool was still of value, and before shearing became no more than an addition to the flock's annual health plan, lamb was a rarity and most sheep meat was mutton. A four-year-old, black-faced, heather-reared wether, properly hung, tastes just like the finest venison. I have always kept a few wethers on each heft to lead the ewes out of snow and to ensure that we have some of this exquisite succulent meat every year. Mutton can still be found in certain specialist butchers and, because a roast will be bigger than lamb, it needs to be carved slightly differently from lamb.

Determine whether you have a right or left leg as the thickest meat will be on the outside. For a right-hand leg, insert the fork in the meat well up the roast at its thickest part on the left. The pelvic bone is on the underside and the first cut should be made across the roast at its thickest part down to the bone, leveling the knife when the edge of the meat is reached on either side. Make the second cut 1/4 inch (5mm.) parallel with the first, angling the knife to free the slice. Proceed, taking slices on either side of the original cut, until this side has been finished. Turn the meat, reposition the fork, and proceed as before.

shoulder of lamb

A fiddly thing to carve, a shoulder of lamb, but worth the effort. Shoulder meat, because of its bone content, is the sweetest cut.

As with a leg, positioning the fork depends on whether you are carving a left or right shoulder. For a right shoulder, insert the fork into the flesh above the blade bone. The bones, if you can imagine them, are now in a zig-zag formation with most of the meat in the cusp of the zig-zag, facing away from you. Cut deep down to the bone on the left next to the shoulder—a little probing with the tip of the carving knife establishes where the shoulder stops and meat begins. Make another cut $1/5$ inch (4mm.) to the right of the first, and change the angle of handle and blade to remove the slice. Continue carving until the meat has been removed from the cusp made by the angle of the bones.

Move your fork back slightly so that it is firmly fixed in the edge of the meat, above the blade bone, and carve slices from the shallow meat covering the shoulder blade. Now, turn the shoulder over, reposition the fork and carve slices along the bone towards the fork. Next, move the fork forward to hold the roast in place so that slices can be carved from the knuckle end.

1 Carve straight through and down to the shoulder bone in $1/5$ inch (4mm.) slices.

2 Take the slices down to the shoulder blade.

3 Turn the roast over and slice horizontally.

saddle of lamb

A whole saddle of lamb always makes the carver tremble a little. It is an impressive, expensive joint, containing the finest meat on the carcass. Trusler referred to it as a "genteel and handsome dish," and the occasion for serving it is usually pretty important. Take heart: In reality it is only the rump and two racks from the shoulder to the pelvis, joined together by the backbone, with the fillet and kidneys underneath, protected by the fatty flanks.

While the wife schmoozes the boss, the carver has three separate parts of the joint to carve—the rump, saddle, and fillet— and, bearing in mind how quickly lamb fat coagulates, he needs to move rather fast. To do the job properly and with style, the carver must have plenty of room to maneuver theroast and a clear idea of the sequence of cuts. On each plate there should be a slice of rump, saddle, and fillet.

Inserting the fork in the roast near the backbone on the left-hand side, run the point of your knife down the length of the backbone until the blade meets the hip bone. Turn the knife and run the blade straight down beside the hip bone over the rib. You now have a clear right-angled incision separating the chop meat from the rump.

Make another incision $1/5$ inch (4mm.) thick parallel with the first, angling the blade towards the top bone when you meet the rib bones. Lift out a delicious long pink strip of meat and lay carefully on the plate.

Move your fork to the left-hand side rump and insert. Carve a slice across the roast toward the hip bone. This will be fatty, so discard, and repeat, adding the slice of rump to the plate.

Now, making sure that your fork is firmly in place, turn the whole roast over. This could be the moment for a quick flurry with the steel. The boss, who will doubtless be an electric-carving-knife sort of fellow, will be terribly impressed. Cut away the protecting flank neatly and discard. Remove the kidneys and carve along the fillet toward the top bone. Add to the plate with a spoonful of juices and perhaps a slice of the kidney fat containing a sliver of kidney.

1 Run the knife along the backbone and over the ribs.

2 Carve $\frac{1}{5}$ inch (4mm.) slices parallel with the backbone. Take slices either side of the rump.

3 Turn the roast over and carve the fillet.

1 Remove the top bone and carve $^1\!/_2$ inch (1cm.)
slices in line with the ribs.

2 Carve $^1\!/_4$ inch (5mm.) slices parallel with the ribs.

rack of lamb

A rack of lamb is the chop meat on one or other side of the backbone and there are three possible ways to carve this cut. With a rack from a big sheep, ask the butcher to remove the chine (top) bone, giving the carver unobstructed access to the meat.

Carve 1/3 inch (1cm.) slices in line with the chop bones, freeing the meat by cutting between it and the bone.

Another way, particularly for a small roast, is to carve slices parallel with the chine, angling the knife away from the chine when the blade touches the rib. Continue carving slices 1/4 inch (5mm.) thick over the ribs. These long strips of meat will be much more acceptable and pleasing to the eye than a plate full of little circular pieces.

A third way is to ask the butcher to saw through the chine between the middle of each chop rib and simply cut down, through the chine and the tissue that joins the ribs. In this way you will be serving individual chops that have been cooked as a whole roast.

3 Separate the individual chops from the joint.

crown roast of lamb

hindquarters of lamb

I always think a crown roast of lamb something of an unnecessary gimmick. There is a touch of Belle Epoque about the end of each trimmed chop bone decorated with its individual little paper frill, a hint of Edwardian decadence. But I can see that it still has a place today at something like a special occasion for a child. That last lunch before going back to school, or a birthday, perhaps.

A crown roast is simply a rack of lamb bent in a circle with the meat inside, tied up with string. The middle is filled with vegetables, peas maybe, or mashed potato. The butcher will have carefully divided each rib where it is attached to the chine bone and carving a crown is simply a matter of cutting between each chop bone and serving each individual chop with its paper frill and a spoonful of whatever has been cooked in the middle. The young will love the novelty of it.

This delightfully extravagant cut is usually seen only with young lamb, and is the rear half of the rack where it joins the pelvis, containing the loin, kidneys, and legs. The tail is usually split and the kidneys mounted on the two ends just before cooking is complete so that they are not overcooked.

Divide the saddle from the legs by severing them from the pelvis where the ball-shaped joint joins the pelvis. Lay aside on a separate platter, and carve each as per the instructions for leg and saddle, serving a couple of slices of each on individual plates, with a tiny piece of kidney and a sliver of fillet.

A challenge in the carving line, which I would not recommend to any but the most experienced carver.

lamb cuts

Oh Lord, when hunger pinches sore
Do thou stand us in stead
And send us from thy bounteous store
A tup or wether head. Amen.

A Burn's night grace from the Globe Tavern, Dumfries

1 Leg and shank end
2 Loin and saddle
3 Rump and fillet of leg
4 Loin chops and chump chops

5 Scrag end of neck
6 Shoulder, middle neck
7 Breast and belly

veal

choosing and cooking veal

Veal is a meat people have been brainwashed about. It is the natural by-product of the dairy industry: If you want milk, cheese, and cream, which are produced when a cow has calved, you must remove the bull calves, because there isn't enough for both. Beef cattle are usually the product of a suckler herd. The types of cattle raised for milk production don't make particularly good beef, but they are great for veal.

Eating veal is no different from eating spring lamb. We don't crate veal in the U.K. as they do on the Continent, so there is no possible complaint of cruelty. Veal as I buy it is a healthy pale pink with a white fat covering and is quite delicious. Very few U.K. butchers sell it, but most will gladly get it on demand.

loin of veal stuffed with its own kidneys

Get your butcher to bone out a loin of veal and roll it around its own kidneys. You must use lard for this dish to make the most of it, but if you quail, use vegetable oil. It is a dish that I think my sister Heather invented, and it is very good indeed.

Serves 4–6

$2^{1}/_{4}$–$2^{3}/_{4}$ pounds (1–1.3kg.) boned loin of veal
$3^{1}/_{2}$ tablespoons (50g.) lard
6 onions, chopped
salt and freshly ground black pepper
$2^{1}/_{2}$ cups (600ml.) red wine

Heat the oven to 375°F (190°C).

In a heavy flameproof casserole or Dutch oven, heat the lard and gently fry the onions until slightly colored. Place the meat on top of the onions, season with salt and pepper, and pour over the wine. Cover and cook in the oven 1 hour. Remove to a warm place, deglaze the casserole, and serve the juices with the meat. If liked, you can add a little cream to the sauce, and heat it through gently before serving.

roast veal

People tend not to think of veal as a roasting meat, and indeed it is more usually found as chops or escalopes and in blanquettes, but a good veal source will produce a very good and not too large roast. I tend to use loin, either on or off the bone, although a leg cut is also good. Veal tends to dry out very quickly, so it must not be overcooked. If it does not have a good layer of fat, then cover it with fatty bacon. I like to spread the surface of the joint with Dijon mustard because I think this goes very well without swamping the flavor. I also lard it with anchovies and/or bacon.

A 2¼–3 pounds (1–1.3kg.) roast will serve 4 to 6 people.

Heat the oven to 375°F (190°C).

Cook the roast in the oven 15–20 minutes per pound (500g.), depending on whether it is on or off the bone.

carving veal

Veal has never been a traditional or popular meat in Britain. The Saxons would only have killed a calf if something was wrong with it, and the fact that the Normans ate veal with gusto merely confirmed the prevalent view that they were horrid foreigners with nasty habits. The European practice of bleeding calves at slaughter during the Middle Ages, and its association with Jewish slaughtering practices, created further xenophobic prejudice.

More recently, the sale of bull calves to farmers who reared them as export veal was both an important component of dairy farming and an essential form of diversification. Pressure from animal welfare groups brought a ban on the live export of veal calves and imposed such draconian restrictions on rearing them that the British veal industry has effectively ceased to exist and thousands of bull calves are now incinerated every month. Veal is still available from specialist butchers. The meat is close-textured and moist, and all joints are carved like the equivalent cuts of lamb or, for a bigger roast, mutton. Remember that your knife must be very sharp.

For a small roast, holding the knuckle end in the left hand, remove a wedge-shaped piece of meat by cutting down across the bone nearest the knuckle. Proceed to slice the meat directly across the roast down to the bone, angling your knife slightly to the right to avoid undercutting. For a larger roast, steady it by inserting the fork at the pelvic end. Make the first cut at the widest part of the joint by inserting the knife at the far side and cutting through to the bone, leveling the knife parallel with the serving platter as you cut over the joint. Like lamb and mutton, proceed to take slices on either side of the original cut ¹/₅ inch (4mm.) thick, angling the knife as you reach the bone to free them. When one side is carved, turn the roast and carve the other side.

tongue

choosing and cooking tongue

hot or cold tongue

I love tongue and it is an almost totally lean (if you care for that sort of thing) meat, far less daunting to cook than you think and readily reusable, to say nothing of delicious. An ox tongue can weigh up to 4½ pounds (2kg.), with a calf's tongue half that weight. Lambs' and pigs' tongues are much smaller. You can put your tongue in brine or pickle before cooking.

Ox (beef) tongue has an outstanding flavor. I shall give you an ox tongue recipe to eat hot or cold, but you can use yummy little lambs' tongues equally. Try it and see. For braised tongue simply blanch the tongue 10 minutes in boiling water, then drain and braise in the oven with wine and vegetables 45 minutes per pound (500g.) at 350°F (180°C).

A 4½ pound (2kg.) tongue will serve about 12.

1 ox tongue
1 large onion
1 bouquet garni (bay leaf, thyme, parsley, rosemary)
a few pinches of coarse or kosher salt
a handful of black peppercorns

Place the tongue in a large saucepan, add the other ingredients, and bring slowly to a boil. Skim and simmer gently until the tongue is very tender, allowing 45–60 minutes per pound (500g.). Remove the tongue from the liquid. Cool until you can handle it, then trim away the fat and bones from the root. Make a small incision at the tip of the tongue and peel away the skin; you may have to cut it away at some parts.

If you are eating the tongue hot, slice it and reheat it in your sauce. For cold, curl it with the tip in the center into a circle and place in a bowl, a soufflé dish is good—or a small saucepan to hold it in shape. Place a plate on top and weight it down. Leave it like this overnight or for 24 hours in a cool place before serving. Serve it with a wine or fruit sauce, or I like it with parsley sauce. Cumberland sauce is also good.

carving tongue

I am very partial to tongue, particularly when it has been salted. Boiled and served with mustard sauce, it makes a delicious old-fashioned dish, rarely seen nowadays. A tongue can come to the table in two ways: rolled and pressed or pinned with skewers, or *au naturel*. I think it is better served hot *au naturel*, providing the tongue is a decent size.

A cold tongue is better served rolled and pressed. This will be carved across the horizontal like a small rolled beef roast. Insert the fork in the left-hand side of the tongue about an inch (2.5cm.) from the top, flange raised, and carve slices $\frac{1}{8}$ inch (3mm.) thick across the tongue towards the fork, moving the fork lower as carving progresses. About halfway down, begin to angle the knife so that one side of the tongue is higher than the other. As you near the bottom, place your fork upside down and carve over the fork. The last few slices may look slightly uneven but you will have used all the meat.

The hot tongue will be sitting up on the serving dish, so insert the fork into the top and, holding firmly, carve slices $\frac{1}{4}$ inch (5mm.) thick across the tongue from the tip back toward the fork.

Hot tongue
Carve in $\frac{1}{4}$ inch (5mm.) slices.

Cold tongue
Carve horizontally.

About halfway through, begin to angle your knife.

pork

choosing and cooking pork

The art of choosing pork is to remember that roast pork is indigestible without its fat, and that crackling is one of the world's great joys. The meat should be a good rich pink: too red and it won't taste as good; too gray and it will taste as it looks.

For a loin of pork you will want a fair covering of fat, no less than the length of the first digit of your thumb and no more than the whole thumb. The fat should be creamy white and the rind, which will provide the crackling, a pinky yellow. This is not as easy as it sounds. The U.K. Meat and Livestock Commission, which is obsessed with lean meat, has driven the pork industry into ruin by demanding they produce very lean pork. The end result is that pigs are killed far too young, so young in fact they don't even bother to castrate the boars, and they have developed no flavor and no fat.

It has become so bad that outdoor pigs actually get sunburned. There are, however, some good producers , and pressure on your own butcher will help. Pork suppliers actually do give an option of breeds, and I find Berkshire or Middle White to be the best types for oven-roasting, while Gloucester and Tamworth are better for the pot-roasting recipes.

There are various roasting cuts of pork, loin and leg (ham) being the preferred cuts. Loin is a drier meat, and it is vital not to overcook it as it can go like cardboard. It provides the best crackling to my mind. Leg is juicier and again it is important to have a covering of fat (although rather less than on the loin), but without it you won't get crackling.

There are also the cheaper and often forgotten cuts. These are hand and spring, shoulder, sparerib, and belly. The hand (picnic ham or shoulder) is the bit below the knee and above the foot. It is delicious, with lots of crackling, but requires quite careful cooking. Sparerib should be cooked as for leg. Shoulder I find better for potroasting, and belly is very good rolled and stuffed and responds well to both methods.Some of these cuts are not traditionally found in the U.S.A.

Crackling

The real secret of the crackling is in the scoring. Ideally your butcher will do this for you, but if this isn't possible use a scalpel or a utility knife rather than a kitchen knife. Score the loin about $1/8$ inch (3mm.) deep and across its length in narrow strips. For other cuts, cross-hatch this to provide tiny squares which will crackle beautifully. Rub the rind first with salt and then with oil, rubbing the salt in (in the words of the late Fanny Cradock, a pioneer U.K. celebrity chef) as if into the face of your worst enemy.

roast pork

The best way of straight oven-roasting is to put your prepared joint on a rack in the oven tray. Heat the oven to 475°F (240°C). Roast the pork at this temperature 20 minutes, then reduce the heat to 350°F (180°C) for the remainder of the cooking time, between 20 and 30 minutes per pound (500g.) This will depend on the cut and the amount of bone (which will obviously speed cooking). A 2^1/$_2$ pound (1kg.) roast will serve four to six.

I, however, use Fanny Cradock's method, which is to roast for the whole time in a preheated oven at 425F° (220°C) about 23 minutes per pound (500g.)

portuguese roast pork

The Portuguese are great pork eaters and cook it in many ways, even famously with clams. This is one of the few recipes for a roast, and it is very good, especially for the rather lean, poor pork which is often all that is available.

Serves 4–6

2^1/$_4$ pounds (1kg.) piece of boneless pork loin
^{1}/$_2$ stick (50g.) butter
^{1}/$_2$ cup (125ml.) white wine
4 cloves
4 black peppercorns
salt
1 bay leaf

Heat the oven to 350°F (180°C).

Place the pork in a baking dish, smear the butter on top and pour the wine around the edges. Add all the other ingredients to the wine, and roast the pork in the oven 1^1/$_2$ hours or until brown. Baste from time to time.

Remove the rind before serving.

brazilian roast sucking pig

The first time I ever ate sucking pig was in Brazil when I was about five, and it remains a favorite of mine. Once, when sailing in the West Indies, a friend refused to allow me to buy a sucking pig from those that were running about on the beach, so I promised her to have a party when she was next in London. I cooked six sucking pigs in my ovens all sitting up facing each other and finished them off on a spit.

Serves 8

1 sucking pig (also known as suckling pig), about 12–14 pounds (5.5–6.5kg.), liver, kidneys and heart reserved
1/3 pound (150g.) bacon, sliced

Marinade
1 garlic clove, crushed to a paste
2 tablespoons each salt and freshly ground black pepper
1 tablespoon cloves
2 bay leaves
2 1/2 cups (500ml.) each red wine vinegar and red wine
1 teaspoon cumin seeds

Stuffing
1/4 pound (125g.) bacon, chopped
1/3 pound (150g.) smoked ham, chopped
1/3 pound (150g.) smoked sausage, chopped
2 garlic cloves, crushed
2 tablespoons olive oil
1 onion, chopped
1 bunch of scallions, chopped
1 tablespoon chopped parsley
1 cup (200g.) semolina, cooked in twice its bulk of water
2 hard-boiled eggs, shelled and chopped
5 ounces (150g.) whole green olives, pitted

Mix the marinade ingredients together, pour over the piglet, and leave to marinate 24 hours, turning occasionally. Keep the marinade when you remove and dry the piglet.

To make the stuffing, fry the bacon, ham, and sausage with the garlic in the oil, then add the reserved variety meats. Brown, stirring continuously, and adding small amounts of water as it gets dry. Cook about 30 minutes until all the meats are tender. Add the onion, scallions and parsley, and continue to fry until the onions are browned. Add the semolina, stirring continuously until well mixed. Remove from the heat and add the eggs and olives. Taste and adjust the seasoning. Stuff this mixture into the piglet and sew up.

Heat the oven to 400°F (200°C).

Put the piglet in a roasting pan, cover with the bacon slices, and cook in the oven 20 minutes. Reduce the heat to 350°F (180°C) and continue to roast for a total of 12–15 minutes per pound (500g.) Baste with the strained marinade every now and again.

hungarian stuffed belly of pork

The Hungarians, according to George Lang, their great cookery authority, have more pork recipes than any other nation, and this despite their cattle-based agriculture. Belly of pork is a very cheap cut but very delicious for all that. If you like you can increase the amount of paprika—the classic flavoring of Hungary—in the stuffing here. Traditionally the dish is served with a potato and onion salad.

Serves 4–6

2¹/₄ pounds (1kg.) belly of pork
1 teaspoon salt
3¹/₂ tablespoons (50g.) lard
1¹/₄ cups (300ml.) stock

Stuffing
2 white rolls, soaked in about ²/₃ cup (150ml.) milk and
   squeezed well
2 eggs
¹/₃ pound (150g.) each pork liver and bacon, roughly chopped
1 onion, finely chopped and fried in a little lard to soften
1 garlic clove, crushed
¹/₂ teaspoon each ground black pepper, paprika, and
   dried marjoram

Heat the oven to 325°F (160°C).

Bone the meat and cut a long pocket in the middle between the layers of meat.

Mix all the stuffing ingredients together well and season with 1 teaspoon of the salt. Put the stuffing evenly into the opening in the meat and sew up.

Melt the lard in a roasting tin. Rub the remaining salt over the meat, then roast in the oven in the heated lard, basting regularly until it is brown and crisp, about 2–2¹/₂ hours. Remove the pork.

Pour the fat from the pan, deglaze it, and make a gravy with the stock.

roast hand and spring

This is a very cheap cut—indeed at one time Harrods would give it to you for nothing, because they did their own butchery and were glad to be shot of it. Like so many cheap cuts, it needs a bit more care, but is an excellent meat.

Serves 6–8

1 hand and spring (or picnic ham), about 3 pounds
  (1.3kg.), boned
salt and freshly ground black pepper

Stuffing
1 onion, chopped
1 tablespoon lard or vegetable oil
1 tablespoon sage leaves
1/2 pound (225g.) pork sausage meat
1 teaspoon ground ginger
2 cups (125g.) fresh white breadcrumbs
1 egg

For dredging
3/4 cup (50g.) fresh white breadcrumbs
1 small apple and 1 onion, grated
1 teaspoon chopped sage

Heat the oven to 375°F (190°C). Score the rind of the roast. For the stuffing, sweat the onion in the fat, covered, for 5 minutes, then add the sage. Remove from the heat and blend with the rest of the stuffing ingredients. Stuff the pork with this, then fold in the ends. and tie with butcher's string. Roast in the oven about 1³/4 hours. Mix all the dredging ingredients together, rub over the meat, and roast another 15 minutes or so to brown before serving.

pork in milk

This is a traditional French method of cooking pork, and of course dairy-fed pork is supposed to be particularly tender and succulent.

Serves 6–8

3 pounds (1.3kg.) loin of pork, boned, rolled, and
  crackling removed
1/4 stick (25g.) butter
1 quart (1 liter) whole milk
2 carrots, sliced
1 onion, quartered
1 garlic clove, peeled
1 bouquet garni (thyme, bay leaf, and parsley)
salt and freshly ground black pepper

Heat the butter in a deep, heavy pan and brown the pork all over. Add enough milk to cover completely. Add the carrots, onion, garlic clove, bouquet garni, and salt and pepper. Cook uncovered over a very low flame 3 hours, adding more milk if necessary. Serve with its own sauce.

loin of pork from jerez

Jerez is the sherry-producing capital of Spain and this larding of pork with ham and cooking with sherry is traditional to the region. The Spanish were enthusiastic pork eaters in the days of the Inquisition. It was the surest way of winkling out the Marranos (converted Jews) or the followers of Islam who were covert non-Christians.

Serves 6

2¼ pounds (1kg.) loin of pork, boned and skinned
2 ounces (50g.) raw (prosciutto type) ham, cut into strips
3 tablespoons stock
⅔ cup (150ml.) sherry
salt and freshly ground black pepper
12 small onions, peeled

Heat the oven to 375°F (190°C).

Get your butcher to bone and skin the pork; keep all the trimmings. Lard the interior of the pork with the ham strips (use a larding needle if you have one). Roll and tie the roast with the fat outside. Put the rind and trimmings in the bottom of the pan and put the pork on top. Surround with the bones, pour over the stock and sherry, season, then roast in the oven, basting occasionally, 30 minutes.

Put the onions round the pork and cook for a further 15 minutes. Raise the oven temperature to 400°F (200°C) and cook for another 15 minutes.

Remove the string from the pork and transfer to a carving dish, surrounded by the roast onions. This is traditionally served with fried potatoes.

pork stuffed with prunes

Prunes go very well with pork, and this is a combination found in many European countries. Here is a traditional French version.

Serves 4–6

2¼ pounds (1kg.) loin of pork, boned and crackling removed, or fillet
1 pound (500g.) small prunes
½ stick (50g.) butter
salt and freshly ground black pepper
6 cooking apples

Soak the prunes in water overnight and pit them. Make incisions in the pork and insert the prunes, leaving 6 for the apples, then chill in the refrigerator for 8 hours.

Heat the oven to 425°F (220°C).

Spread the meat with a little butter and roast in the oven for 1 hour, basting as you go. After 20 minutes, season with salt and pepper.

Peel and core the apples, leaving a band of skin around the middle, and insert a prune and a piece of butter into each. Bake at 300°F (150°C) 1 hour. If you have only one oven, bake the apples first and keep them warm.

Carve the meat and serve with the apples.

rack of spareribs

Hardly a challenge in the carving department, but a rack of spareribs makes a spectacular lunch dish—especially if barbecued on a hot summer's day.

Serves 4

1 large rack of pork spareribs

Sauce
2 tablespoons each tomato ketchup, Worcestershire sauce, hoisin sauce, soy sauce, and olive oil
2 garlic cloves, smashed
2 teaspoons mustard
1/2 teaspoon brown sugar

Mix all the sauce ingredients together, spread them liberally over the rack, and leave 2 hours.

Preheat the oven to 400°F (200°C).

Place the pork on a rack in a roasting pan and cook in the oven about 20 minutes (or cook on your barbecue).

garlic roast pork

The Scots and French manner of cooking pork removes the rind, which is then used in soups and casseroles. This of course leads to an absence of crackling, so it is important to buy good pork with a covering of fat.

Serves 4–6

2$^{1}/_{4}$ pounds (1kg.) loin of pork (without its rind), or piece of leg
2 garlic cloves, slivered
1 teaspoon each dried oregano, thyme, and rosemary, crumbled
2 teaspoons English mustard powder
3 tablespoons olive oil
salt and freshly ground black pepper

Mix the garlic with the herbs. Make incisions in the surface of the meat and insert the herb-laden garlic slivers. Mix the mustard with the oil and salt and pepper and brush over the meat. Leave to rest 1 hour.

Heat the oven to 375°F (190°C).

Wrap the meat in foil and cook in the oven 1$^{1}/_{2}$ hours. Turn off the oven and leave the meat to rest therein 15 minutes. Unwrap and carve thinly. This is very good served cold for a buffet.

roast pork boulangère

carving pork

Traditionally housewives with no oven would take dishes to be cooked in the baker's oven. This all-in-one dish is traditional to northern France.

Serves 6

3 pounds (1.3kg.) loin of pork, boned and rolled
6 potatoes
3 apples
1/2 stick (50g.) butter
salt and freshly ground black pepper
1 large sprig of rosemary

Heat the oven to 350°F (180°C).

Peel the potatoes and apples and cut in thick slices. Dot an ovenproof dish with the butter, then place the apples in the dish with the potatoes on top. Place the piece of pork, well tied, on top. Season with salt and pepper, then scatter the rosemary leaves across the meat.

Roast in the oven 1 hour, basting as you go. If the meat browns too fast, cover with foil. Serve in the dish in which it is cooked.

One of the great beauties of food is the mental images its taste and smell invoke. Close your eyes as you eat an oyster in England and there is the gray sea at Whitstable, the crash of surf, and the rattle of a pebble beach. Cut into the breasts of a teal and you have the gradually closing gap as the gloaming merges with dark, the sudden "whish" of wings, and the bang of a gun. The smell of roast pork is definitely leaves turning from green to yellow gold, the reds and scarlets of rose hips and rowan berries, and the musty scent of autumn. Or at least it used to be. Most pork I see in the average butcher's makes me think of wet concrete, and the stuff you see in supermarkets, with its sanitized square of added pigskin, the utility area at the back of a hospital.

The standard of the vast majority of pork meat sold today is a glaring example of the damage supermarkets and legislation are capable of wreaking on the unsuspecting public. A pig is supposed to be fat, but the fast-food culture has created an animal that produces meat tasting like chewy blotting paper. The law that forbids a pig to be kept near a house, another urban law imposed on the rural population, destroyed the rural man's traditional diet, and there is now a whole generation who don't even know what real roast pork tastes like. Thank God, the tide is on the turn, and in the U.K. an ever-increasing number of specialist pig breeders is producing the real thing.

leg of pork

In the happy event of being asked to carve a whole leg of pork, or indeed any pork roast, the carver should have access to a sharp kitchen knife or even a pair of pruning shears for removing sections of the crackling. Never risk blunting your precious carving knives trying to cut through tough, brittle skin. Crackling may be delicious, but it can wreak havoc on those carefully maintained edges.

Armed with these, the carver has two options. One is to proceed as with a leg of lamb—at the shank end and carving up the leg. The other way is as for a leg of mutton or large leg of lamb. Starting well up theroast at the fleshiest part, remove a broad section of the crackling by cutting through it well over on either side of the joint. Crackling out of the way, slice across and down to the bone, leveling the knife as the edge is reached on either side, taking $^1/_5$ inch (4mm.) slices on either side of the original cut. I prefer this method. A leg of pork is for a large party and by starting in the middle and working outward you insure that each guest receives a slice from the fatter rump and the leaner shank end.

Shank-end half legs

With a shank-end half leg of pork, proceed exactly as you would for a shank-end gigot joint of lamb and the same for a rump end (see pages 48–49).

Finally, I should mention shank-end and rump-end half joints. Carve these from the point where the butcher has divided the roast back towards the knuckle for a shank end and back toward the tip of the pelvic bone structure for a rump end.

sucking pig

The chances of being asked to carve a sucking pig are probably infinitely remote, but just think how awful it would be if one were and couldn't. Anyway, the secret of a successful life is to be prepared for any eventuality. That's what Baden Powell used to maintain.

The wee pig is presented to the carver covered in all sorts of nonsense: flowers, fruit, leaves, and what-not. Not to mention the apples stuffed in its mouth and a pair of cherries in the eye sockets. This wants getting rid of and, once it has, the business of carving can start.

Insert the fork horizontal to the pig and behind the left shoulder. With the blunt edge of the carving knife, tap the skin round the shoulder. This, being very crisp, will break away easily, exposing the flesh underneath. Cut around the shoulder down to the joints. The piglet is very well cooked and the whole foreleg should come away easily. If there is any resistance, take hold of the trotter and twist as you probe with the knife point. Move the fork to the top center of the hind leg and cut away. Repeat on the other side.

Now, try to lift as much crackling off the body in a whole piece as possible. Place on a separate wooden platter and cut or break into convenient pieces for serving.

With the body of the pig exposed, either carve slices parallel to the backbone or, if the pig is big enough, at right angles to the backbone, in the same way as for a rack of lamb.

loin of pork

1 When the roast is presented to the carver the chine (top) bone will have been sawn through by the butcher where it is attached to the rib bones. Run the knife along the chine between the meat and the bone, and remove.

2 Work from left to right to remove a segment of crackling and place this on an adjacent wooden platter ready to be reduced to suitable pieces per plate.

3 Slice off the upper corner of meat so the edge of the joint lies at an angle of 30 degrees.

4 Carve slices $1/5$ inch (4mm.) thick across the roast and down to the rib bones, turning the blade to free each slice. Maintain the angle of the meat throughout.

ham

choosing and cooking ham

I am not concerned here with the uncooked hams of the Parma or Cumbrian air-dried type, because it is highly unlikely that you will buy a whole ham of this nature and take it home. If you do, though, you will carve it in exactly the same way as a cooked ham. Such hams are more used for cold buffets or appetizers than for main meals and are excellent with fruit.

This is perhaps a good place to mention mutton ham which is still served at the Moonlite Diner in Owensboro, Kentucky. It needs to be cooked like a pork ham, and has a very unusual flavor which is better suited to my mind to being reheated, sliced, in cassoulets or such dishes. At one time hams were produced from a variety of animals, from beef, venison, and even badger.

There are very few types of cured hams for cooking now available to buy in the U.K.. When I was young you could choose between York hams, Bradenham hams, treacle-cured hams, and many others. In some hams the difference is in the cure, in others the smoke. It is generally accepted that a York ham is the sweetest and most succulent. It is so called because when the great Minster was being built the locals used the oak chippings from the huge beams to smoke their hams. Yorkshire is a county which probably understands pork better than anyone, still having pork butchers and even a very serious pork pie contest, and a good York ham is hard to beat. Some butchers and people like my friend Peter Gott, the wild boar expert, cure their own hams, and many butchers brine their own gammon and cure their own bacon. Johnny has been searching for a Bradenham ham these last eight years to no avail.

Always buy your ham on the bone. Many suppliers will send you a cooked ham, and perfectly good they are too, but to my mind this removes half the fun. Eschew the boneless ready-cooked hams of the deli counter whenever you can. Always ask if and for how long a ham needs soaking before cooking, although nowadays they are not cured with so much salt.

boiled ham

baked ham

Don't be overawed by the thought of cooking a ham: It isn't difficult if you remember certain rules. There is an almost ritualistic feel about cooking a large ham. I remember my brother and I cooked one every Christmas, usually in cider, and would sit up half the night watching it, topping up the liquid, and generally putting the world to rights. You don't have to do this, but it is fun. In Ireland it is traditional to have a ham for funerals, and I have left in my will instructions as to who will cook mine!

When you buy your ham, make sure it has a good covering of fat and that the area around the bone is clean of any discoloration or mortification. Ask your butcher whether the ham needs soaking before cooking. If you do need to soak it, leave the ham overnight in a basin of cold water under slowly running water to save you changing the water every few hours. If the ham is very salty, put it in cold water, bring slowly to a boil, then throw away the water and start again. A 6½ pound (3kg.) ham will feed about eight to ten.

To cook your ham, put it in a container large enough to hold it. Place it on the stove and fill with cold water, then add a handful of cloves and peppercorns, several bay leaves, and 2 tablespoons of brown sugar. If you like, you can cook your ham in dry hard cider or even apple juice. Most important is that when you are cooking a ham you must not let it boil.

Put it over a medium heat and bring it slowly to a boil, for about 30 minutes. Watch it carefully at the end of this time, and as soon as the first bubble breaks the surface, turn the heat right down. Cook the ham 20 minutes per pound (500g). When the ham is cooked, the rind will pull off easily. Remove this carefully and stud the fat of the ham with cloves. Coat the surface with toasted fine breadcrumbs.

If you would like to finish your ham in the oven, boil it for two-thirds of the time, remove from the liquid, and carefully cut away the rind. Stud with cloves and spread with one of the glazes given on page 79. Then transfer the ham to a heated oven at 325°F (160°C) and cook for the remainder of the time.

It is also possible to cook the ham entirely in the oven, in which case wrap it in foil and bake at 375°F (190°C) for the calculated time. About 15 minutes before the end, remove the foil, cut off the rind and glaze, then return to the oven for the remaining 15 minutes.

ham stuffed with apricots

Ham stuffed with apricots is a medieval dish from Oxfordshire, probably adapted from a recipe brought back from the Crusades. This dish was traditionally served at the St. Giles Wool Fair.

Serves 6

4¹/2 pounds (2kg.) ham, bone removed
¹/2 pound (250g.) pitted apricots, chopped, or ¹/4 pound (125g.) dried apricots, soaked
4 cups (250g.) fresh white breadcrumbs
salt and freshly ground black pepper

Glaze
apricot jam mixed with a little hard cider and English mustard powder

Heat the oven to 375°F (190°C).

Mix the apricots and breadcrumbs together, season and bind with a little water. Stuff into the cavity in the meat, then wrap the meat in foil. Cook in the oven 1³/4 hours. Remove the foil, anoint with the glaze, and cook another 15 minutes.

ham in a huff

The only person I know who still cooks ham this way is my yoga teacher, the renowned Mary Stewart, who comes from Leek in Staffordshire. It produces a delicious juicy ham and is well worth the effort. You do not eat the flour-and-water paste, which is a direct descendant of meat cooked in a pastry "coffin" in the Middle Ages (large pans were in short supply then). It works for any size ham, but I have used just a small piece.

Serves 6

4¹/2 pounds (2kg.) ham
3¹/2 cups (500g.) all-purpose flour

Soak the meat at least 4 hours, then dry.
Heat the oven to 375°F (190°C).

Mix the flour with enough water to give an elastic dough (1 –1¹/4 cups/250–300ml.). Roll out to ¹/2 inch (1cm.) thick, wrap carefully around the ham and secure all the edges well. Bake in the oven 25 minutes per pound (500g.), plus an extra 15 minutes.

Break the huff at the table for maximum dramatic effect.

Glazes
2 tablespoons (50g.) molasses mixed with 4 tablespoons beer
3 tablespoons marmalade, melted
1 small bottle ginger ale and 1 tablespoon English mustard powder
2 tablespoons (50g.) clear honey mixed with 2 tablespoons red wine vinegar, then dredge with ¹/2 cup (125g.) brown sugar and baste with sherry.

carving ham

Pork is synonymous with autumn when, traditionally, pigs fattened through the summer and finished on windfall apples were killed; hams are synonymous with Christmas. They are also an epicurian link with the great pagan winter festival of Yule, celebrated with such uninhibited enthusiasm by our Celtic forebears.

Salt mining and salting meat for winter consumption were specialities of the Celts, and hams are a surviving legacy from a period for which there are few historical records. The extravagances of the festive season—goose, turkey, plum pud, candied fruit—are eclipsed by a ham on the bone, lovingly cured in the months from killing to Christmas. It is by far the most luxurious of the gastronomic excesses and, paradoxically, the least wasteful. Everyone loves ham and is still happily eating it long after cold turkey or goose has palled. And, finally, the bone will make a delicious pot of soup.

Of all the British cured hams—the mild subtle Wiltshires, robust Worcesters, classic Yorks, and sweet Suffolks—Bradenhams or black hams (as they are now called since the company that held the Bradenham name ceased trading) are without doubt the connoisseur's ham and, sadly, very hard to find. Very mature, and cured for longer than any of the other hams in a mixture of molasses and juniper berries, the flesh is firm and claret-colored with a unique sweet flavour and long after-taste. It was one of these, sent down from Paxton and Whitfield in London's Jermyn Street, that reposed with an unmistakable air of superiority, balanced on a ham stand and covered with a muslin cloth, on the sideboard every Christmas when I was a child.

Most hams, except those especially cured for the Christmas market like black hams, are available all year round, and there are two options for carving them. I use one at Christmas because the body of the ham remains tidier, and the other slightly less wasteful method for the rest of the year.

An essential requirement for carving ham on the bone, to insure thin, even slices, is a sharp, stiff, thin-bladed knife, 10 inches (25cm.) long and $1/3$ inch (1cm.) wide, slightly curved towards the point.

To carve a Christmas ham, take a firm hold of the shank and cut straight down across the thickest part of the flank to the bone. Make the next cut $1/8$ inch (3mm.) to the left, angling the knife slightly to the right so that the blade intercepts the first cut at the bone. With the aid of your fork, lift out this thin, wedge-shaped slice. Now take slices, cutting well over each side of the flank, from either side of the original two cuts. This will give your guests an even distribution of both lean and fat ham, the shank being the leaner and flank the fatter. Gradually the center of the ham will come to resemble an extending V. Slices should be slightly less than $1/8$ inch (3mm.) thick.

To carve a ham at other times of the year, start at the shank end, taking out a small wedge of meat to enable carving to proceed at an angle of 25–30 degrees. At the same time take slices straight down on the vertical along the right-hand side of the shank. When the shank is finished proceed to the tail, carving inwards towards the crown. Eventually the two will meet and your ham will be finished.

Pork cuts

There is another way, which I mention only because the Reverend Dr Trusler includes it in his book of 1788, and I have never seen it anywhere else. With the point of the carving knife, carve a small circular hole in the center of the flank, taking out and discarding this small piece of meat. Proceed, cutting thin slices in an ever-expanding circular direction. The purpose of this, according to Trusler, was to preserve the juices and prevent them running out. The Georgians were very enthusiastic about juices and it would certainly have kept the ham moist, the juices remaining trapped in the ever-expanding hole.

A hot ham on the bone, either a whole or half leg, is carved in exactly the same way as pork or lamb.

A boned and rolled ham is carved as you would rolled beef or any other rolled joint, with your knife angled slightly to the left to avoid undercutting.

The Baptist found him far too deep;
The Deist sighed with saving sorrow,
And the lean Levite went to sleep,
And dreamed of tasting pork tomorrow.
Winthrop Mackworth Praed

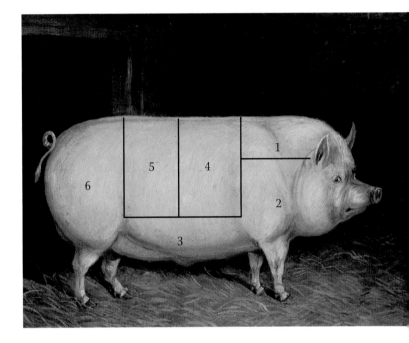

1 Spare ribs
2 Hand
3 Belly
4 Fore loin
5 Hind loin
6 Fillet, leg, and knuckle

poultry

chicken

choosing and cooking chicken

More people eat chicken than any other meat, and yet most people have never tasted real chicken. The reason so many recipes for cooking chicken contain long lists of ingredients is to overcome the fact that the majority of chickens sold don't taste of anything, except perhaps polystyrene! There is a variety of reasons for this, the predominant one being that the average bird is raised over a mere five weeks from egg to table, and has no time to develop any flavor. (A number of producers now sells at eight to ten weeks, but shop around and you may find even longer rearing periods.)

Promise me you will buy cage-free and check very carefully to see that it isn't merely packaged in the U.S.A.. In Thailand they have two E.U.-licensed packing and dressing plants, very confidence-boosting until you realize that the chicken comes under E.U. regulations only at the very moment of death, and heaven knows what happened to it or what it ate until that moment. I could tell you horror stories that would make your hair fall out about chicken production around the world, but trust me and I shan't.

The trend for chicken breasts has caused chicken producers to crossbreed into strains that are bigger breasted to produce more meat in this area. There is no harm in this since crossbreeding of domestic animals has continued throughout history, coming to a head at the time of the eighteenth-century Agricultural Revolution. Outside a supermarket, choosing a chicken becomes a matter of personal choice rather than just one of weight: You need to think who at your table likes what, and then choose the bird accordingly. Some producers will sell you carcasses and giblets separately and quite cheaply which is great for making more stock (don't have qualms about making stock with both cooked and uncooked carcasses together because stock is always well boiled). Occasionally you can get hold of a stewing chicken, which is an old bird, often an egg-producing hen that has stopped laying. They have a lot more flavor, but will require longer, slower cooking, and are not suitable for roasting.

There are a few producers who raise chicken properly, and the taste is fantastic. Earlier this year I cooked one of these for a BBC researcher who was amazed, and said sadly that in another generation no one would recognize it as chicken.

roast chicken

poached chicken

There are two separate time calculations. A properly raised cage-free chicken takes 20 minutes per pound (500g.), and the rest about 12–15 minutes per pound (500g.). If you are stuffing the bird, add another 20 minutes. A 2³/₄ pound (1.3kg.) bird will feed four.

Heat the oven to 450°F (230°C). I tend to cut the trussing on an unstuffed chicken; otherwise the breast is cooked before the legs. Put a ¹/₂ onion or lemon inside the bird, plus a piece of fresh rosemary, thyme, marjoram, or oregano and about a tablespoon (15g.) butter. Rub the bird with salt and pepper and smear with some more softened butter (or pour over some oil). Put in a roasting pan, place in the oven, and cook 15 minutes before reducing the heat to 325°F (160°C) for the remainder of the calculated cooking time. Baste once or twice during cooking. To test that the bird is done, stick a sharp knife into the thickest part of the thigh. If the liquid comes out clear and not pink, the bird is cooked. If the juices are pink, cook 10 more minutes and test again.

A simple way of cooking, and one that helps the bird to absorb flavor. If the bird is young, it is a good idea to wrap it in cheesecloth or tubular stockinette before poaching (this stops it falling apart).

The bird should be stuffed and trussed, then placed in a pot or saucepan and covered with water or stock. Add some salt and bring slowly to a boil, skim, then add a couple of sliced leeks, carrots, and small onions, a bouquet garni and, if liked, a whole head of garlic. An old bird will need 2 hours to poach, so if you are serving the vegetables with the bird replace them 30 minutes before the end of the cooking time. A young bird will take about 1 hour. Instead of serving the broth as soup in the case of a young bird, strain it and make a velouté sauce or a sorrel sauce before serving.

A strange variant but one that works is a Chinese method where you put three solid silver spoons into the bird, place it in the stock, bring it to a boil, and allow to boil 10 minutes. Turn the heat off and leave the pan tightly covered for the chicken to "cook." This is very good if you want the bird cold, or you may carve it when it is cooked and reheat in a sauce.

chicken casserole from the Canaries

basic stuffed roast chicken

4 pound (1.8kg.) chicken, cut into 8 pieces
flour
3/4 cup (150ml.) olive oil
1 medium strong onion, chopped
1 garlic clove, finely chopped
2 cups (500ml.) dry white wine
1¼ cups (300ml.) chicken stock
1 bay leaf
1/2 teaspoon dried thyme
1 teaspoon ground saffron
15 blanched almonds, finely chopped
1/2 cup (25g.) coarse fresh breadcrumbs
2 hard-boiled eggs, chopped
4 tablespoons finely chopped parsley
salt and pepper

Season the flour and coat the chicken pieces with it. Heat two-thirds of the oil in a heavy pan and sauté the onion and garlic until soft. Add the chicken pieces and sauté, turning regularly until just golden. Pour in the white wine and enough stock to barely cover the chicken. Adjust the seasoning and add the bay leaf and thyme. Cover and simmer about 45 minutes or until the chicken is tender.

Dissolve the saffron in a little hot water and add it and the almonds to the chicken. If the sauce looks too thin, cook uncovered for a little longer. Fry the breadcrumbs in the remaining oil until crisp and brown. Put the chicken pieces on a serving dish and sprinkle with the breadcrumbs, chopped hard-boiled eggs, and parsley before serving.

There is something very exciting about a whole roast chicken brought to the table—to me it evokes scenes of harmony and abundance quite out of keeping with its reality.

Serves 4

2³/4 pounds (1.3kg.) roasting chicken
1/2 stick (50g.) butter, softened

Stuffing
3 slices bacon, chopped
1/4 stick (25g.) butter
1 onion, chopped
1¹/2 cups (75g.) old bread, roughly crumbled
1 large bunch of herbs (to include chopped parsley)
finely grated zest and juice of ¹/2 lemon
1/3 cup (75ml.) sherry or wine
1 egg
salt and freshly ground black pepper

Heat the oven to 450°F (230°C). For the stuffing, in a large skillet fry the bacon in the butter, then add the onion, and fry until soft and golden. Add the breadcrumbs and cook until they have taken up all the fat and colored slightly. Add the herbs, lemon zest and juice, and the sherry or wine, and allow to cool. Break the egg into a small bowl and beat well, then add to the mixture. Stir in well with a fork to distribute evenly, then season to taste.

Stuff the inner cavity of the bird and use a skewer to close, or sew up. Put the bird in a roasting pan, smear with butter, and roast (see page 94) about 1¹/3 hours.

chicken with anchovies

In this recipe the stuffing is spread under the skin of the bird, a technique which can also be done with softened and flavored butter, thin slices of lemon, slices of mushroom, or, as a *tour de force*, slivers of truffle. It won't work with a non-cage-free bird because the skin will split. Anchovies are to me the taste of the Georgian age and I am very fond of them.

Serves 4

2³/₄ **pounds (1.3kg.) chicken**
6 anchovy fillets, washed, dried, and chopped
3 ounces (75g.) bacon, chopped
2 tablespoons chopped parsley
1 onion, finely chopped (even better, use 2 shallots)
salt and freshly ground black pepper
freshly grated nutmeg
pork fat for barding
¹/₂ cup (125ml.) poultry stock

Mix two-thirds of the anchovies, the bacon, parsley, and onion, and season well with salt, pepper, and nutmeg. Insert your hand under the loose flap at the noncavity end of the chicken, loosen the skin, and then slide the stuffing under the skin. Put the bird in a roasting pan and lay the fat over the top. Roast as described on page 84, but at the higher temperature 30 minutes, then at the lower temperature a further 20 minutes.

Leave the bird to rest while you deglaze the pan. Add the stock and the remaining anchovies to the juices left in the pan, and stir and heat to make a sauce.

lemon chicken

This is a traditional Greek method of cooking chicken and is quite delicious. You almost can't have too much lemon, and the dish should be served with rice or "hylopittes," a type of flat white noodle found in Greece (but in their absence, pasta will do).

Serves 4

2³/₄ **pounds (1.3kg.) chicken**
4 tablespoons olive oil
salt and freshly ground black pepper
1 large onion, finely sliced
3 carrots, sliced
1 celery stick, with leaves, finely sliced
6 sprigs of basil
2 lemons
1¹/₄ cups (300ml.) hot water

Heat the olive oil in a flameproof casserole and brown the seasoned chicken all over. Remove the chicken and sauté the onion until it becomes transparent. Add all the remaining vegetables and the basil and sauté for a few more minutes.

Return the chicken to the pan atop the vegetables and pour over the juice of the lemons. Cut the lemon zest into very thin strips and add to the dish. Add the water and more seasoning, cover, and cook slowly 1 hour. Serve.

chicken casserole

This is just a basic chicken casserole, but the variants are endless and can be chosen to suit your palate, your pantry, and your purse.

Serves 4

2³/₄ pounds (1.3kg.) chicken
¹/₂ stick (50g.) butter
1 tablespoon olive oil
2 onions, chopped
2 garlic cloves, crushed
2 teaspoons tomato paste
¹/₄ cup (50g.) pitted olives
salt and freshly ground black pepper
²/₃ cup (150ml.) red wine or strong beer, or the same
   amount of stock if you don't use alcohol
a dash of balsamic vinegar
a handful of thyme or marjoram, chopped

If cooking in the oven, heat the oven to 350°F (180°C).

Heat the butter and oil in a heavy flameproof casserole, brown the chicken all over, and remove (this should take about 10 minutes). Gently fry the onions and garlic until soft in the fat remaining in the casserole, then add the tomato paste, and cook gently a few minutes before adding the olives. Return the chicken to the casserole and sprinkle on some salt and pepper. Pour over the liquids—the alcohol or stock and the vinegar—cover, and cook on top of the stove or in the oven about 1¹/₄ hours. Sprinkle with the herbs just before serving. Serve with rice or something to mop up the juices.

poussin farci au riz

Poussins (spring chickens) are funny little birds, but very succulent and good for one person. When I am alone I smother them in Thai sweet-and-sour paste mixed with some oil and stick them in the oven at 350°F (180°C) 20 minutes to have hot or cold. But this is the classic French way with them.

Serves 4

4 spring chickens or poussins
¹/₄ cup (50g.) long-grain rice
4 teaspoons turmeric or a pinch of saffron
salt and freshly ground black pepper
5 tablespoons olive oil
³/₄ stick (75g.) butter

Cook the rice in a pan of salted water to which the turmeric or saffron has been added, until just tender. Drain thoroughly, and season. Use to stuff the birds and close the openings with skewers.

Heat the oil and butter in a deep flameproof casserole. Brown the birds well all over. Sprinkle with salt and cover. Cook over a low heat on top of the stove 15–20 minutes. Serve hot or cold.

poached chicken with rice

This is such a lovely comforting dish, really best done with a stewing chicken or young cockerel, but still nice with a proper chicken.

Serves 6

4 pounds (1.8kg.) chicken, preferably an old one, trussed
2 carrots, sliced
2 onions (1 studded with a few cloves)
1 large leek, trimmed and chopped
1 bouquet garni
salt and freshly ground black pepper

Rice
$^1/_2$ stick (50g.) butter
1 small onion, chopped
1 cup (225g.) long-grain rice
2 cups (450ml.) chicken stock, reserved from poaching

Sauce
$^1/_4$ stick (25g.) butter
1 heaping tablespoon all-purpose flour
freshly grated nutmeg
4 tablespoons light cream
1 egg yolk

Put the chicken with its vegetables, bouquet garni ,and seasoning in a large pan, cover with water, bring to a boil and simmer gently 1$^1/_2$–2 hours until the bird is tender.

30 minutes before the end of cooking, start the rice. Heat the butter in a pan, add the onion, and cook until golden. Add the rice and stir gently to coat all the grains. Remove 2 cups (450ml.) of the hot stock from the chicken and add to the rice, bring to a boil, cover tightly, and cook 20–25 minutes until all the liquid has been absorbed by the rice.

While the rice is cooking, make the sauce. Melt the butter and add the flour to make a roux. Cook gently for a few minutes. Remove 1$^1/_2$ cups (350ml.) stock from the chicken and start to add it to the roux a little at a time, stirring well, until the sauce is smooth and thickened. Season with salt, pepper, and nutmeg, and cook gently 10 more minutes. Mix the cream and egg yolk together. Remove the sauce from the heat and stir the cream mixture in. Return the pan to a low heat and heat through gently but don't boil (or the egg yolk will scramble).

Put the rice on a serving dish, carve the bird, and place on top. Pour over half the sauce and serve the remaining sauce in a gravy boat.

carving chicken

During my farming life the single most exciting event has been the establishment and ongoing growth of farmers' markets. They are a wonderful advertisement for an industry desperately in need of some good PR, a bright star of hope for the many families seeking to diversify and, at last, a readily available source of decent farm-reared chickens. Mass-produced chickens bear no resemblance in flavor, flesh quality, or bone structure to cage-free ones. These are horrid things to carve because the flesh tends to collapse, but what I find really sinister about them is that the bones are so soggy, you could practically feed them to a dog without fear of splintering. Don't ever do that with a chook bought from a farmers' market.

There is a statistic somewhere that chicken is the most frequently eaten meat in the British Isles. Unfortunately, very little of it is carved. Most is either hacked to pieces with a thing like a miniature chain saw, or quartered with pruning shears. Such a pity.

1 Position your bird with the drumsticks away from you. Insert the carving fork into the thick inner part of the left-hand drumstick and lever away from the body. Cut down between body and drumstick until you feel bone. Lever again to expose the thigh joint and cut through with the knife's point. Sometimes a bit of twisting away is required, but once the joint is freed, cut round the curvature of the body on either side of the joint. Separate the drumstick and thigh, cutting through at the joint. If the bird is a big one, cut slices off the thigh.

2 Remove the wing, cutting through the joint as close to the body as possible without touching the breast meat.

3 Turn the roast so the parson's nose is towards you. Insert the fork to the left of the breast bone and carve a slice from the breast where the body curves around to the point of the wing joint. Continue carving slices starting at 1/2 inch (1cm.), narrowing to a point as the meat is freed. Alter the angle of the knife to follow the curvature of the body. When one side has been carved, repeat the process on the other side, and don't forget to give someone the wishbone.

turkey

choosing and cooking turkey

carving turkey

Being in the catering business I have probably cooked more turkeys than most people who on average cook only one or two a year, so my method is fairly foolproof. Traditionally turkeys were boiled or poached before being finished off on a spit to brown. Having once cooked a totally cage-free turkey I can see why, since they can get very muscular. My friend Donald Dixon has his turkeys running about all summer and they need poaching first. This method is quite close to the original; cooking in foil is really steaming.

Go to a good butcher and ask for a bronze turkey because the flavor is much better, although properly raised white turkeys can be quite good. Avoid the ready-basted variety. (The large white was developed for the American catering market and some of them were so large that the cock couldn't cover the hen. Since this was before the days of artificial insemination, a special mounting saddle was invented!) At Christmas it is a good idea to use an oven thermometer because the temperature may drop with everyone roasting at the same time. A 11 pound (5kg.) turkey will serve eight to ten.

Roast Turkey

Stuff the cavity with a green herb stuffing and use a Sausagemeat or Chestnut Stuffing (see pages 151–153) under the skin at the neck end. Heat the oven to 350°F (180°C) . Lay the turkey on a large piece of foil. Season with salt and pepper and smear with 2 sticks (225g.) butter. Wrap the turkey and cook in the oven 10 minutes per pound (500g.) if the stuffed bird is more than 14 pounds (6.5kg.), 15 minutes per pound (500g.) if less. Some 15 minutes before the bird is cooked, turn back the foil, dredge the breast with flour, and turn up the heat to (220°C) 425°F to brown the bird.

Usually, by the time the festive bird arrives on the sideboard, everyone is exhausted. The young have been on the go since dawn and are tired, fractious, and sated with chocolate. Their parents, up half the night wrapping presents and then dragged from the arms of Morpheus to join in the fun of opening stockings, are at breaking point. The elderly, used to meals at regular hours, have drunk too much sherry and are beyond caring. It is up to the carver to hold the whole thing together, so carve with speed and efficiency.

Carving a turkey is exactly the same as carving a chicken (see page 90), with certain minor differences. See that there is a separate wooden board on hand to carve the darker drumstick and thigh meat, once they have been separated. The breast is usually stuffed with sausagemeat, and slices should be carved across the front of the bird.

As with a chicken, carve the breast straight down with the knife angled at 10 degrees to the breast bone. As the slices get bigger, keep an eye that the point of the knife and the handle are in line. It is all too easy to find that the point is carving at $1/8$ inch (3mm.) and the handle at $1/2$ inch (1cm.). Pity the poor carver on Christmas Day—the young are always ready for more just as he sits down...

fillet of turkey with cherries

This recipe is based on one in Elena Molokhovet's *A Gift to Young Housewives*, which I had been told was the world's unluckiest cookery book, because it was published as the "Mrs Beeton of Russia" in August 1917... Work it out! Sadly, I now learn that this is an apocryphal story as the great Alan Davidson, researching his magnificent *Oxford Companion to Food*, discovered that the four-volume edition had been in print since 1861 and it was only the shorter edition that came out in 1917!

1 have altered the dish so that the fillet is flattened, filled, and rolled, which is better for a buffet.

Serves 6

1 turkey breast, about 2³/₄–4 pounds (1.3–1.8kg.)
1¹/₄ cups (75g.) fresh breadcrumbs
1 egg
¹/₄ stick (25g.) butter
²/₃ cup (150ml.) Madeira

Cherry purée
2 pounds cherries, pitted (keep the pits), or
  3 x 14 ounce (400g.) cans cherries, drained
2 cloves
¹/₂ cinnamon stick
2 cardamom pods
¹/₂ teaspoon freshly grated nutmeg
1 tablespoon superfine sugar

Heat the oven to 350°F (180°C).

Make the cherry purée first. Put the pitted cherries in a pan, add the spices, and simmer gently, covered, until tender. In a separate pan boil 15–20 of the reserved cherry pits in ²/₃ cup (150ml.) water for about 10 minutes, then strain and add the sugar. Add this liquid to the cherry purée.

Trim the turkey breast carefully to remove any tendons, and flatten so that it can be stuffed and rolled. Mix about half of the cherry purée with the breadcrumbs and bind with the egg. Spread this over the flattened breast, then roll up, and tie into a neat shape. Use half the butter to grease a large piece of foil, then place the turkey on it.

Drizzle on the Madeira, and add the remaining butter in small pieces. Close the foil loosely, put the foil package in a casserole dish, and cook in the oven for about 30–40 minutes. About 15 minutes from the end of cooking, open the foil to allow the top of the turkey to brown a little. When the turkey fillet is cooked, place it on a bed of the remaining cherry purée and surround with triangles of white bread fried in butter.

goose

choosing and cooking goose

"A silly bird the goose, too much for two and not enough for three," as the saying goes... They must have had hearty appetites. Certainly there is not as much meat on a goose as would first appear, as it has a very heavy carcass, but it is delicious eating and you do have the bonus of a lot of goose fat to keep for roasting spuds and other such luxuries. The lowest incidence of heart attack is the goose-rearing area of France, far lower than the olive oil regions!

In Spain they serve pears cut in half and cooked in the goose fat 30 minutes in the oven with the goose. Before serving the pears, which are drained of the fat, they pour brandy over them and set them alight. Jennifer Paterson and I were once bidden to cook a goose dinner for the high heid yins [top brass] of the BBC under John Birt, and we served goose stuffed with foie gras. Very rich!

roast goose

Calculate the cooking time of the stuffed bird at 20 minutes per pound (500g.).

Serves 8

10 pounds (4.5kg.) goose
salt and freshly ground black pepper
fresh herbs to garnish

Stuffing
2 pounds (400g.) potatoes, peeled, blanched, and diced
2 onions, chopped
2 tart apples, chopped
3 tablespoons chopped parsley
2 tablespoons chopped sage

Heat the oven to 375°F (190°C).

Mix all the stuffing ingredients together and season with salt and pepper.

Place the stuffing in the cavity and truss the goose. Rub the bird with salt and prick it all over with a fork. Place on a rack in a roasting pan and pour 1 cup (225ml.) boiling water into the pan. Roast in the oven for the calculated cooking time. Baste during cooking. Turn the goose so that it browns evenly. Remove the fat with a turkey baster or pipette during the roasting process because a great deal is given up. (Let it cool and set, pour off the excess water, then use the fat for frying.) Serve the goose with giblet gravy and an apple sauce (the "luxury" one is good—see page 134), and garnish with fresh herbs.

carving goose

The ancestor of our posturing, neurotic, white farmyard goose is the wild graylag, probably the first fowl to become domesticated in the British Isles. During the Middle Ages, goose farming was a major industry, upon which the might of our army depended—the longbow needed goose feather flights for its snowstorms of arrows. Goose grease had an infinity of veterinary and medicinal uses, was the basis for primitive face creams, softened and waterproofed leather, and is, to this day, the finest of all cooking fats.

Geese grazed on pastures through the summer and fattened on the gleanings left by reapers after harvest were the traditional festive winter bird, and thousands were walked to market in London, their feet dipped in tar to enable them to make the journey. Except for a few Scots die-hards who still celebrate Hogmanay with one, turkeys have completely deposed geese as the Christmas bird, and geese have become sadly neglected. A pity, because a young goose makes a really rich and delicious dish—and think of all that lovely fat...

Position as for a chicken (see page 90) and, prising the thigh open, cut into the thigh joint. This will almost certainly be very stiff and require taking hold of and twisting. Remove the thighs and drumsticks, which are exceptionally sinewy and should be set aside for deviling or converting into confit at a later date. Do the same with the wings.

Turn the carcass so that the thigh bone is toward you and make an incision down the length of one side of the dividing breast bone. Make a second incision exactly parallel with the first, between $1/8$ and $1/4$ inches (3 and 5mm.) from it, turning the blade in toward the breast bone as it nears the bone and cutting inward, freeing the slice. Continue carving

in this manner until the flat bone drops down toward the wing and thigh joints. Here the carver changes the position of the knife for the last few slices and carves straight down over the curvature of the bird.

At one time, rabbit legs were included in the stuffing for a goose. These would absorb some of the goose's flavor. Not as rich as goose flesh, they were ideal for children.

duck

choosing and cooking duck

The only duck you will easily get in Britain is the Aylesbury duck, which was a large white duck reared traditionally as a cottage industry (in wooden boxes hung on the cottage walls!). However, it will probably now be called Norfolk duckling: when a survey of duck producers was carried out in the late nineteenth century it was discovered that there were no commercial duck rearers outside Norfolk.

There are also Gressingham ducks, which have been raised for a larger breast, and Muscovy (Barbary) ducks, which come from France and were originally raised for pressing. You may find it hard to buy duck at all unless you have a good butcher. All these breeds can be obtained in the U.S.A.

Don't buy frozen branded ducks because they will fall apart on you. The birds tend to be raised in such a way that the carcass and meat do not blend well together. Look for a bird with a good bone structure, meat on the breast, and a good pink color inside the cavity.

Carving duck

Domestic ducks are carved in exactly the same way as geese. If they are well cooked, the drumsticks and thighs can also be served.

roast duck

This simple recipe was my mother's invention. It is quite delicious and on one occasion when we served it at home, Boris Chaliapin, the son of the great Russian opera singer, ate a whole duck all to himself, much to my youthful annoyance because the dish is just as good cold as hot.

Serves 4

4 1/2 pounds (2kg.) duck
2 handfuls of salt
2 handfuls of superfine sugar

Heat the oven to 350°F (180°C).

Rub the duck vigorously all over first with handfuls of salt and then of sugar. It is important to do it in that order.

Stand the duck on a rack in a roasting pan and pour a little water underneath. Roast in the oven 2 hours, basting every 30 minutes.

duck with orange

duck paillard

A great classic dish, ruined for anyone my age by ghastly treatment by bad chefs, but worth revisiting.

Serves 4

4½ pounds (2kg.) duck
¾ stick (75g.) butter
salt and freshly ground black pepper
1¼ cups (300ml.) poultry stock
⅔ cup (150ml.) dry white wine
1 veal knuckle, sawn in pieces
5 oranges

Heat the butter in a large, flameproof casserole and brown the duck on all sides over a moderate heat. Season and add the stock, wine, and veal bones. Cover and simmer 2 hours.

Remove the duck from the pan and keep warm. Strain the sauce and skim off the fat. Return the sauce to the pan and add the juice of 2 of the oranges and their zest cut into thin strips. Boil 2 minutes.

Put the duck on a platter and garnish with the remaining oranges, cut into slices. Reheat the sauce and pour over the duck. Serve with rice.

A robust French dish.

Serves 4

4½ pounds (2kg.) duck, including liver
6 shallots
½ pound (200g.) fat pork belly
salt and freshly ground black pepper
1 stick (100g.) butter
1¼ cups (300ml.) full-bodied red wine
1 bouquet garni (thyme, bay leaf, and parsley)

Heat the oven to 450°F (230°C).

Chop 3 of the shallots and half the duck liver together. Shred the pork belly, and mix with the liver mixture. Season, stuff into the cavity of the duck, and sew up.

Spread the duck with half the butter and roast 15 minutes per pound (500g.)

Chop the remaining shallots and liver, and put in a pan with the wine, bouquet garni, and some salt and pepper. Cook until the mixture has reduced by a quarter, stirring well. Just before serving, remove the bouquet garni, add the remaining butter in small bits, and whisk vigorously. Carve the duck and serve with the stuffing surrounded with the sauce.

peking duck

What everyone orders in a Chinese restaurant, you can now do at home and amaze your friends. This duck is normally served with pancakes, julienned cucumber, scallions, and hoisin sauce. The vodka replaces the traditional rice spirit, which can be hard to find and not much different.

Serves 4–6

5 pounds (2.25kg.) duck
2 teaspoons salt
1/2 cup (125ml.) vodka
4 tablespoons clear honey
2 cups (450ml.) hot water

Pancakes
2 1/4 cups (225g.) all-purpose flour
3/4 cup (175ml.) boiling water
1 tablespoon sesame oil

To serve
hoisin sauce
julienned cucumber
scallions, cut into short strips

Remove the fat from the cavity of the duck. Slice off the tail, and remove the oil glands on either side of the tail bone. Rinse the duck inside and out, and dry with paper towels. Rub the inside of the duck with salt, put on a large plate and spoon vodka over it, rubbing well all over the duck. Leave for 4 hours, turning occasionally. Dissolve the honey in the hot water and brush over the duck, ensuring no spot is missed. Hang on a rack in the wind or in front of a fan for 4–5 hours; I use a hairdryer on cold.

Heat the oven to 400°F (200°C), and place the duck on a rack in a roasting pan lined with foil for reflection. Pour in 1 inch (2.5cm.) of water and cook in the oven 30 minutes. Reduce the heat to 350°F (180°C) and cook a further 1 1/2 hours, or until the skin is golden brown.

Meanwhile, make the pancakes. Put the flour in a bowl and pour on the boiling water, stirring with a chopstick or wooden spoon handle until it is cool enough to handle. Knead 10 minutes until the mixture is a soft, smooth dough. Form into a ball, wrap in plastic wrap, and rest at least 30 minutes. Roll into a cylinder and cut into eight equal slices. Cover to prevent drying. Taking one slice at a time, cut in two, and form each into a ball. Flatten into 3-inch (7.5cm.) circles and brush the tops with oil. Place one on top of the other, oiled sides together. Lightly flour a rolling pin and work surface and roll the joined pair into a circle to form a thin pancake approximately 6 inches (15cm.) in diameter, turning over at least once. Repeat with the remaining seven slices. Cover as you make them. Cook the pancakes on an ungreased nonstick griddle over a low heat until small bubbles form. Turn as you go so the pancakes cook on both sides until just browned. Very carefully separate the two layers, making two pancakes from each pair. Stack these, browned side upward. Cover with plastic wrap to prevent them drying out. Cover and reheat in a steamer over boiling water.

Serve the duck, both flesh and skin, shredded—and you don't need Johnny to tell you how to do that. Each diner takes a pancake, spreads it with hoisin sauce, adds a little cucumber, scallion and shredded duck, then rolls it up, and eats.

yorkshire christmas pie

Nowadays this is referred to as a "bird in a bird," but this is the correct name. In the Middle Ages the dish was cooked and brought to table in a huge pastry "coffin," the sides of which had been filled in with pieces of moorfowl and hard-boiled eggs. I wrap mine in puff pastry to cook, and it used to be a feature of parties when I cooked at Rebeka Hardy's pheasant shoot dinners.

It takes huge patience boning out the birds, but otherwise is not so difficult. I used to separate the larger birds with different colored stuffings, but now I think the variant colors of meat are enough. You can ring your own changes, but this is one version.

You will need a long sharp flexible filleting knife and a small very sharp knife. I used to use one of my grandfather's surgical scalpels.

Serves about 20

1 pigeon
1 partridge
1 mallard
1 pheasant
1 small goose
1 small turkey
salt and freshly ground black pepper
4 x 1 pound (450g.) pack frozen puff pastry

Heat the oven to 400°F (200°C).

Carefully bone out each bird. You make an incision along the backbone right to the bone and, using your hands and the small knife, ease back the skin and flesh as closely from the bone as possible. Remove the wing tips and ease the skin and flesh from the wings, then work on the legs and thighs, and finally remove from the breast. Work slowly and tear the skin as little as possible. Start with the smallest bird and, when done, rub the bird all over with salt and pepper. Return the bird to as near to its original shape as possible, then sew up and repeat with the next bird, wrapping this round the first bird and sewing up. Repeat until all the birds are boned and wrapped, the one around the other.

Roll out your puff pastry leaving it quite thick, and wrap it round the bird package. Make a small hole in the top and insert a cone of paper as a chimney. Place on a rack in a roasting pan and cook in the oven 20 minutes per pound (500g.) until the pastry is golden brown (cover with foil if browning too much). Alternately you can use foil instead of pastry, and rub the top bird well with butter. This dish can be served hot or cold.

duck with cucumbers

I have recently been making a program on Georgian food centered on the work of Hannah Glasse who, in 1747, wrote the best-selling cookbook ever. I am a great fan of both Hannah and eighteenth-century food and this is her recipe, only slightly adapted by me.

Serves 4

6¹/₂ pounds (3kg.) duck
2 cucumbers , peeled, halved,
   seeded, and cut into ¹/₃ inch (1cm.) cubes
1 large strong onion, sliced
²/₃ cup (150ml.) claret-type red wine
flour
salt and freshly ground black pepper
1 stick (100g.) butter
2 teaspoons (10g.) butter mixed with 1 tablespoon flour
1¹/₄ cups (300ml.) veal or chicken stock
1 cup (225g.) rice
1 tablespoon chopped flat-leaf parsley

Put the cucumbers and onion in a bowl, pour over the wine, and let it marinate 2 hours.

Preheat your oven to 400°F (200°C).

Rub the duck all over with flour, salt, and pepper and smear with ¹/₄ stick (25g.) butter. Roast the duck 20 minutes, remove from the oven, and prick all over with a sharp fork, piecing only the skin not the flesh—this lets the fat run out. Reduce the oven to 325°F (170°C) and cook the bird a further 20 minutes, then prick again, and return for another 20 minutes.

While the ducks are cooking, drain the cucumber and onion, reserving the marinade. In a skillet heat ¹/₄ stick (25g.) butter and fry the vegetables until they begin to brown, sift a little flour over them, and after 3–4 minutes stir it in. Season well and put in the flour and butter mixture, pour on the stock and reserved wine marinade, and cook gently 15 minutes.

Cook the rice, drain, and toss in the remaining butter.

Carve the ducks and arrange on a meat plate surrounded by the rice. Place the cucumbers and their sauce over the duck and sprinkle with chopped parsley.

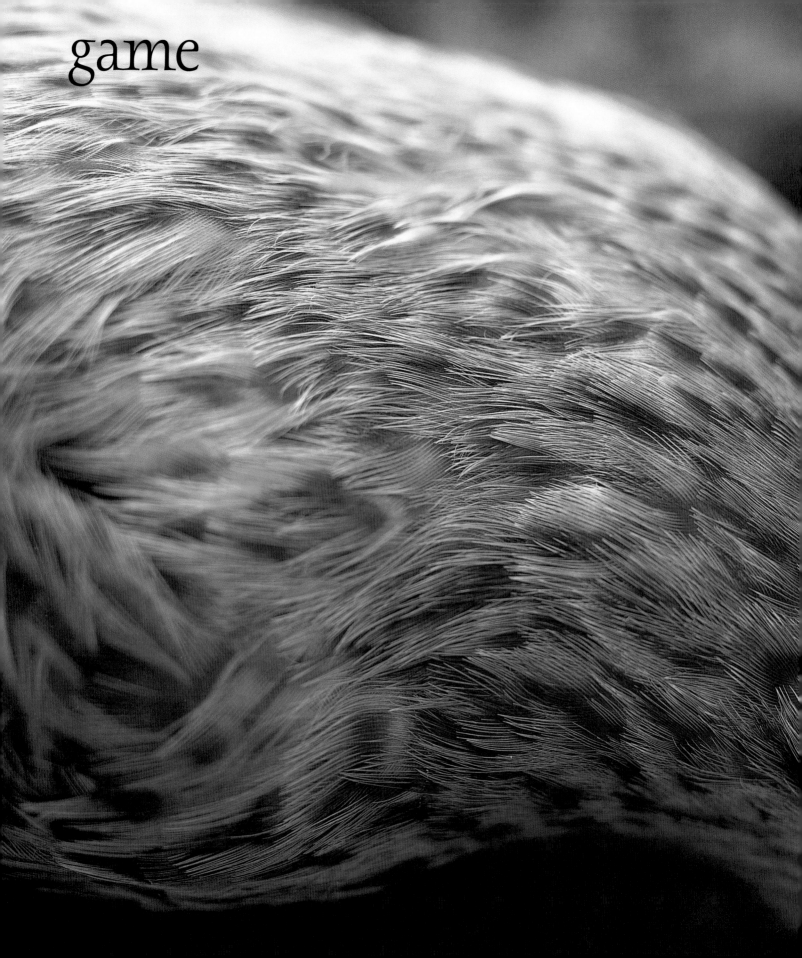
game

game birds: pheasant

choosing and cooking pheasant

pheasant with figs

If you live in the right area there are certain times of the year when they will give you pheasant for nothing. You'll have to pluck it yourself or find a friend to do so, but pheasant is a delicious bird if properly hung, and if you're into lean and outdoors, well, there you go.

Every piece of meat or fowl should be hung to tenderize it and enhance its flavor, and pheasant more than most. A newly shot pheasant is edible but tasteless, and by the next day it is tough and tasteless. It is one of the reasons you don't find much pheasant in supermarkets because they generally don't have the capacity to hang game.

A pheasant should be hung for anything from three days to ten depending on the weather. Forget stories of maggoty pheasant, because that would take a lot longer, and is an acquired taste like very ripe cheese. I don't like either my Stilton or my pheasant at the crawling stage, but I know those who do. Pheasants should be hung suspended from the neck behind a fly screen. To test for readiness, if you pull a tail feather and it comes out easily, the bird is then ready for eating.

This recipe is from the south of France where pheasant and figs are around at the same time. That's not quite so easy to find in the U.K. or U.S.A., so I use figs that have been preserved in wine or brandy. On occasion I have used dried figs that I have soaked overnight in brandy or cold tea, depending on which incarnation I was in!

Serves 2

1 pheasant
1 stick (100g.) butter, plus extra for smearing
salt and freshly ground black pepper
8 fresh figs, peeled, or preserved or soaked dried figs
  as above
3/4 cup (200ml.) game stock
2 cups (450ml.) heavy cream

Smear the pheasant with the extra butter and place the bird in a tight flameproof casserole. If you like, you can add some of the preserving or soaking liquid from the figs. Cook over a low heat 45 minutes, then season with salt and pepper.

In a separate pan, gently stew the preserved or dried figs in the measured butter 10 minutes (fresh only about 3 minutes). Add 2 tablespoons of the stock and the cream and cook for a little longer until heated through.

Remove the pheasant to a dish. Remove the figs from the sauce and arrange around the bird. Deglaze the pheasant pan with the remaining stock, then add the cream sauce. Heat through and pour over the pheasant.

normandy pheasant

This classic dish, combining the two Norman staples of apples and Calvados, always puts me in mind of the Tournament of the Pheasant when all the brave knights of the court came to joust carrying a pheasant each as a sign of fidelity. Why, God only knows, because the only good thing about a pheasant is eating it.

1 pheasant
1/3 cup (50g.) seedless raisins
1 stick (100g.) butter
1 1/2 pounds (650g.) apples (not cookers)
1 1/4 cups (300ml.) heavy cream
juice of 1/2 lemon
2 tablespoons Calvados
1/2 teaspoon ground cinnamon
salt and freshly ground black pepper

Soak the raisins in warm water 20 minutes. Heat half the butter in a large pan and brown the pheasant all over. Remove from the pan.

Peel, core, and thinly slice the apples. Heat the rest of the butter in a separate pan and quickly sauté the apple slices over a high heat so they are browned but not cooked.

Put a good layer of apples in the pheasant pan, place the bird on top and surround it with the rest of the apples. Pour on the cream mixed with the lemon juice, Calvados and cinnamon, and season. Add the raisins, cover and cook over a moderate heat (or in a preheated oven at 325°F (160°C) for 1 1/2 hours.

roast pheasant

If your pheasant is a small wild bird, you will need to halve the cooking time given below.

Serves 2

Heat the oven to 350°F (180°C).

Put a piece of apple in the cavity, season the pheasant, and either bard the back with fat bacon or wrap the bird in foil. Roast in the oven 35 minutes. Unwrap the foil and turn back, or remove the bacon from the breast. Dredge the bird with a little flour, smear with softened butter, and roast a further 10 minutes to brown slightly.

Serve with Bread Sauce (see page 138), unthickened gravy from the juices (see page 129), game chips, and fried breadcrumbs.

game birds: wild duck

choosing and cooking wild duck

wild duck with red cabbage

Wild duck are different from domestic ducks in that they are smaller, the meat is darker and, because they have less fat, are potentially tougher. They need to be cooked either very fast for a short time or quite slowly.

This is a Polish dish, and indeed wild goose or virtually any game bird can be cooked in this manner, as well as farmyard duck or goose, but in the latter case reduce the oven temperature after 10 minutes to 350°F (180°C) and cook the goose a further 40–50 minutes.

Serves 4

2 mallard ducks or varied smaller ducks
salt and freshly ground black pepper
1 medium red cabbage, shredded
1 tablespoon lemon juice
1/4 pound (125g.) salt pork, diced
1 onion, chopped
2 tablespoons plain flour
1 cup (250ml.) red wine
1–2 tablespoons superfine sugar
2 tablespoons caraway seeds

Heat the oven to 425°F (220°C). Rub the ducks inside and out with salt and pepper. Prick with a fork. Place on a rack over a roasting pan and roast in the oven 10 minutes.

Pour boiling water over the shredded cabbage and drain at once. Sprinkle with lemon juice, which will help it keep its color. In a heavy ovenproof pan cook the salt pork over a medium heat until transparent, then add the onion, and cook a few more minutes. Add the flour and stir well, then add the cabbage along with the red wine, sugar, some pepper, and the caraway seeds. Cover and simmer 30 minutes.

Transfer the ducks to the pan with the cabbage, cover and cook 45 minutes on top of the stove until the birds are tender. Serve with boiled potatoes and baby turnips.

game birds: guinea fowl

guinea fowl with peaches

I find guinea fowl more exotic than pheasants or peacocks, with their strange cave-drawing shape, their designer plumage, and their weird cry like a creaking gate. Their eggs are like a practical joke, as hard as china, and at a full moon the birds will keep you awake all night. I am not particularly fond of them to eat, but there are those who love them and this is a very nice recipe. It also uses up that bottle of peach brandy that someone brought, but if you've already drunk it use brandy or Armagnac. In season use fresh peaches for this dish.

Serves 2–3

1 large guinea fowl
2 onions, sliced
3 ounces (75g.) bacon, diced
3/4 stick (75g.) butter
salt and freshly ground black pepper
1 sprig of fresh thyme
1 bay leaf
5 tablespoons peach liqueur
1¼ cups (300ml.) poultry stock
1 pound (450g.) preserved peaches, drained

Heat the oven to 450°F (230°C).

Take a deep casserole and line the bottom with the onions and bacon, then dot with butter, season, and add the thyme and bay leaf. Place the guinea fowl on this and roast in the oven until the bird is browned. Remove from the oven and reduce the oven temperature to 400°F (200°C). Pour the liqueur over the bird and ignite. When the flames subside, add the stock, cover tightly, and cook in the oven a further 45 minutes. Remove the bird to a heated dish and keep warm. Strain the sauce and, if too thin, boil to reduce.

Put the peach halves flat in a large pan, add the sauce, and simmer 3 minutes. Arrange the peaches around the bird and pour over the sauce.

carving game birds

Snipe, grouse, woodcock, partridges, and the smaller wildfowl, like teal, widgeon, and goldeneye, are always served whole, and the carver has an easy time of it.

To take the meat off any of these delicious birds, start with the legs toward you and your fork firmly fixed in the left of the breast bone. Make your first incision along the length of the breast, parallel with the breast bone just above the wing. Cut down, angling the knife to free the slice. You may need a second cut to free the meat where it attaches to the wishbone. Remove the fork and use it to eat. Replace the fork and repeat, moving upwards towards the breast bone after each slice is eaten, until the breast is clean. Turn the bird and repeat. Cut or tear off wings and legs, and eat using the fingers with the same gusto and pleasure as your ancestors.

Mallard and wild goose are carved in exactly the same way as their domestic cousins, by removing legs and wings and carving parallel with and over the breast (see page 95).

Pheasants—and here I grab the opportunity to say how I abhor the habit of skinning and cutting the breasts off pheasants to avoid plucking—are carved just as you would a chicken (see page 90). And there is one tip worth remembering when carving game birds. Do not make the mistake of spoiling the flavor of their meat by assuming, because they are smaller than domestic ducks or chickens, that slices should be carved correspondingly thinner.

game animals: venison

choosing and cooking venison

Venison is the meat of a deer. Although traditionally in Britain it has come to mean red deer, also available for eating and very good are roe deer and fallow. In the U.S.A. there are the larger beasts—the wapeti, moose, and red deer and the smaller—the white-tail deer and mule deer as well as the antelope-like proghorn.

All deer is very lean and must be larded or barded with fat. Potroasting is also good.

For good meat suppliers of game see pages 184–185.

roast shoulder of wapeti deer

Johnny and I were recently "sold" for charity and the titled family who bought us requested this dish. David Lidgate, the President of the Guild of Butchers in the U.K., supplied me with two excellent shoulders of fallow deer between 8 and 8³/₄ pounds (3.6 and 4kg.) each from the Royal Parks, which cooked beautifully and were a great triumph.

Serves 4

1 shoulder of wapeti deer
6 juniper berries
salt and freshly ground black pepper
olive oil
barding fat

Heat the oven to 350°F (180°C).

Crush the juniper berries and mix with some salt and pepper and a little olive oil. Smear over the surface of the meat, then cover with the barding fat. Put in a roasting dish and roast in the oven for 15 minutes per pound (500g.).

marinated haunch of venison

A haunch of venison (the hind leg) makes a fine roast. If the deer is wild, it may take longer to become tender and relax.

Serves 8–10

1 haunch of venison
1/4 pound (125g.) lardons (fat bacon or pork fat cut into thick strips)
salt and freshly ground black pepper
1 sheet of barding fat
1 large onion, chopped
1 celery stalk, chopped
1 bouquet garni (bay leaf, thyme, etc.)

Marinade
4 cups (1 liter) red wine
4 tablespoons olive oil
2 onions, finely sliced
2 shallots, finely sliced
1 celery stalk, sliced
2 each of the following: bay leaves, thyme sprigs, parsley sprigs, and garlic cloves (crushed)

Marinate the venison overnight in the marinade ingredients. The next day preheat the oven to 325°F (160°C). Lard the venison all over—either thread the lardons on to a larding needle and draw it under the skin of the venison, or, using a sharp knife, insert the fat under the skin. Season with salt and pepper and tie the barding fat over the haunch. Put the vegetables and bouquet garni under the venison in a stewing pan or Dutch oven. Pour over the marinade. Cover and roast in the oven 3 hours or until tender. Discard the barding fat and keep the venison warm. Strain the cooking liquid and reduce over a high heat by one third. Serve with the meat.

carving venison

The method of carving any of the different cuts of venison is determined by the size of the carcass, but differs very little from the method for lamb or mutton, and the carver makes his decision when he sees the size of roast.

White-tail or mule-deer venison, in my view the most delicate, is carved like young lamb: the legs from the knuckle end toward the hip and the saddle in strips parallel with the backbone. With the larger deer—wapeti, moose and, red deer—the haunches are carved like a very large leg of lamb or one of mutton. Start in the middle of the meatiest part of the leg and carve outward.

Saddles of mule-deer or white-tail are carved depending on size: smaller ones like lamb, and larger ones as you would a loin of pork or fillet of beef, down from the backbone and over the ribs but in $1/5$ inch (4mm.) slices.

A mighty saddle of red deer, wapeti, or moose is definitely carved like a sirloin and the leg like mutton, but make sure that slices are as thin as possible. There will be no shortage of flavor.

game animals: rabbit and hare

choosing and cooking rabbit and hare

We bury tons of wild rabbit every year in the U.K. because Walt Disney and the memory of myxomatosis have removed a once thriving trade. Wild rabbit remains a good, healthy, lean, organic meat. The same cannot be said of farmed hutch rabbit, most of which comes from China or France, both of which have been guilty of horrors in intensive farming. With the Chinese rabbit the vegetables they feed on are often manured with human "night soil." This is a practice the Chinese have built an immunity to, but we have not. Buy wild and do everyone a favor, including the rabbits.

Roast Rabbit

Choose a large young rabbit for this dish. You can tell a young animal by its ears, which should be flexible and easy to pierce with a fingernail. However, in most cases you will buy it dressed, so go to a butcher you can trust.

Serves 3–4

1 whole rabbit (about 1–2 pounds/ 0.5–1 kg.), skinned and
   head removed
salt and freshly ground black pepper
1/2 stick (50g.) butter, softened
2 tablespoons Dijon mustard
4 tablespoons brandy

Preheat the oven to 375°F (190°C). Season the rabbit, place in a roasting pan, and smear with butter. Roast in the oven 40 minutes or until tender, basting every 10 minutes. About 10 minutes before the end of cooking, brush it with the mustard. Baste at least twice more. Remove the rabbit and deglaze the pan. Pour the brandy into the pan juices and ignite. Pour the juices over the rabbit and serve with polenta and a wine sauce.

carving rabbit and hare

North America has three principal hare species—the black and white jackrabbit, and the snowshoe hare. These have a variety of almost indistinguishable relations, like the tundra or arctic hares of the remote, far northwestern coastal regions, and the antelope hare of the Sonoran and Chihuahan deserts. There are also a number of European brown hares in northeastern US, southern Ontario, around the Great Lakes, and south of the Canadian Shield.

A roast hare or jackrabbit is presented with the legs drawn into the body and secured with wooden skewers. The best meat is on either side of the backbone, and to insure that guests receive an even distribution of meat I like to carve the whole hare on to a serving dish rather than serve guests individually. Remove meat from the back by taking long slices on either side and at right angles to the spine. Detach the hind legs and cut slices parallel with the thigh bone. The fore leg and shoulder are served in one piece. Give guests a mix of meat from the saddle, thigh, or one of the fore legs. The remaining carcass will make a robust game stock.

A roast saddle and hindquarters of rabbit would be carved in the same way as a roast hare.

stuffed roast saddle and hindquarters of rabbit or hare

If you use hare for this dish, it must be a young hare. You must use a good sized wild rabbit. Cut away the front of the rib cage, leaving six ribs of the saddle and the hindquarters. Loosen and remove the backbone between the pelvis and the top of the remaining ribs. Make stock with the removed bones and the head if you have it. Keep the heart and liver for the stuffing.

Serves 4–6

1 rabbit (about 1–2 pounds/0.5–1 kg.) or hare (about 4–5½ pounds/2–2.25kg.)
1 sheet of barding fat (fat bacon)
salt and freshly ground black pepper
1 tablespoon olive oil

Marinade
1 onion, sliced
2 garlic cloves, crushed
1 sprig of thyme
2 bay leaves
1 tablespoon olive oil
1 cup (225ml.) dry white wine

Stuffing
²/₃ cup (175ml.) stock
1 large garlic clove
½ cup (50g.) stale white breadcrumbs
1 tablespoon Cognac
6 ounces (175g.) mushrooms, finely chopped
¼ pound (100g.) lean pork or veal, finely chopped
2 ounces (50g.) pork fat, diced
2 eggs

Mix the marinade ingredients together and marinate the prepared rabbit or hare (as in the introduction) overnight in a cool place. Make a rabbit stock from the offcuts and bones. The next day, remove the rabbit, dry it, and reserve the marinade.

Heat the oven to 450°F (230°C).

For the stuffing, reduce the stock down to ¹/₃ cup (90ml.) by boiling in a pan. Pound the garlic in a mortar or processor, and mix with the breadcrumbs, Cognac, and the reduced stock in a large bowl.

Add the chopped rabbit heart and liver, the mushrooms, and the rest of the stuffing ingredients and mix well. Stuff the saddle and fold over, sewing or pinning together. Lay the rabbit on its back and place the barding fat over the sewn-up area which contains the stuffing. The stuffing should not be too tight because it swells, and the rabbit flesh shrinks, during cooking.

Lie the rabbit, barded-side up, in a shallow ovenproof dish. Tie the back legs together. Season and pour over the olive oil, then roast in the oven 10 minutes. Reduce the heat to 350°F (180°C) and roast a further 1 hour, basting with the pan juices and the reserved marinade every 15 minutes.

Remove the string from the rabbit before serving. Serve with the pan juices, to which you can add some heavy cream if you like.

game animals: wild boar

roast wild boar with cider

Introduced in 1893 to North America, and again to several estates in the South during the 1920s, wild boar escaped and cross-bred with wild domestic pigs. There is now an abundance of this sort of feral beast which provides excellent pork and a testing hunting experience across many southern states. Pig hunting in Alabama is so popular that it has become practically a religion. Razorbacks are a major game species in many southern states.

Carving wild boar

The success in farming the notoriously ferocious and awkward European wild boar is something of a phenomenon. Over the last twenty years a considerable number of enterprising farmers have utilized areas of rough woodland by diversifying into the production of wild boar meat. They have succeeded in providing the public with an unusual alternative meat source which has gained popularity, where ostriches, bison, and guinea fowl seem to have largely failed. In the U.K., wild boar chops, stews, and sausages now appear regularly on restaurant menus and as bar meals in up-market pubs.

A cut of wild boar, usually the leg, loin or saddle, will be much smaller than one of domestic pork. The lean, close-grained meat, with its distinctly gamey flavor, should be carved in the same way as a white-tail deer. Slices from the leg or loin should be 1/8 inch (3mm.) thick. Slices from the saddle carved parallel with the backbone should be 1/5 inch (4mm.) thick.

Boar is so lean that I tend to treat it like venison and marinate it first. You can cook it as the recipe for Marinated Haunch of Venison (see page 111), or in the Hungarian manner with paprika, wild mushrooms, and soured cream (see page 115), but here is an early English recipe with cider. This will translate to venison as well.

Serves 6–8

2³/₄–4 **pounds (1.3–1.8kg.) wild boar joint, either on the**
   bone or boned and rolled
2¹/₂ **cups (600ml.) strong hard cider**
salt and freshly ground black pepper
¹/₂ **cup (50g.) all-purpose flour**
¹/₂ **stick (50g.) butter**
¹/₂ **teaspoon ground allspice**
1 **bouquet garni (bay leaf, parsley, thyme)**
¹/₂ **pound (225g.) onions, chopped**
¹/₃ **cup (75ml.) game stock**

Marinate the meat 8 hours in the cider in a cool place.

Heat the oven to 350°F (180°C).

Drain and dry the wild boar and dust with seasoned flour. Brown the meat in the butter then place in a stewing pan with all the other ingredients, including the cider. Cook in the oven 2 hours. Serve with an orange and watercress salad.

boar in the bakony manner

Hungary abounds in wild boar, and paprika and sour cream are very much the taste of the country. This is a delicious recipe, which works equally well with the lean pork that is such a sad feature of the meat market at present. Do use lard, since you can heat it to a high temperature to brown the meat.

Serves 6

2³/₄ pounds (1.3kg.) loin of wild boar
salt
4 tablespoons (25g.) plain flour
3¹/₂ ounces (100g.) lard
2 onions, minced
1 tablespoon paprika
¹/₂ cup (125ml.) meat stock
1 pound (450g.) fresh wild mushrooms
3 tablespoons sour cream

Dredge the meat with salt and two thirds of the flour. Melt most of the lard in a skillet and brown the meat all over. Transfer to a heavy casserole.

Fry the onions in the same skillet until softened, then drain off the fat. Add 2 tablespoons cold water and the paprika. Cover and cook until the liquid has evaporated. Add the onions to the meat in the casserole and pour in most of the stock. Cover and cook 30 minutes. Add more stock if needed. Clean the mushrooms but leave whole. Cook in the remaining lard 1 minute, then drain, and add to the casserole. Cover and cook another 30 minutes. Add the remaining flour mixed with the sour cream and stir well. Simmer for a few minutes longer, then serve the boar sliced with some of its sauce, and boiled egg noodles to accompany.

fish

salmon and sea trout

choosing and cooking salmon and sea trout

Farmed salmon is now so plentiful and cheap that we find ourselves back in the times when the London apprentices rioted because they were made to eat it more than three times a week. Sadly the salmon in question is of course farmed, and the fish vary enormously in quality. Wild salmon is now very scarce and unless you catch it yourself I would not encourage you to buy it because stocks need preserving. Sea trout, on the other hand, is plentiful and for some reason stocks are on the increase. It is not a farmed fish and to my palate is much more subtle and delicious than even wild salmon.

Most of the salmon I have cooked in my life has been prepared to be eaten cold, and the recipe given below is totally foolproof. There is a horrible tendency to overcook fish, and please don't go there. Unless you live in the United States, you need fear nothing from undercooked fish. The sockeye or American West Coast salmon does have a tendency to worms, but the best way to deal with this is to freeze the fish: this kills the worms. You can then thaw it and not overcook it.

A 6$^1/_2$ pound (3kg.) fish will serve about eight to ten.

Salmon for cold
Place the fish in a large pan and fill with cold water. Add 2 quartered lemons, a handful of bruised black peppercorns, and 2 tablespoons salt. Cut some strips of foil, fold them over four times and lay them under the fish; leave the ends above the fish to use as handles for removing it when it is cooked.

Bring slowly to a boil and allow to boil for exactly 2 minutes (be very precise). Turn off the heat, cover, and leave the fish in the water until it has completely cooled. Remove the fish, skin it on both sides, and place on a large platter. Dress it with cucumber or lemon slices, and serve with Mayonnaise or Hollandaise Sauce (see pages 144 and 146).

Hot poached salmon or sea trout
Prepare your cooking vessel as above, and place your fish in the water. Bring to a boil and cook 6 minutes per pound (500g.). Remove from the hot water, skin, and serve.

Hot salmon or sea trout in the oven
To my mind this is a better way of cooking fish for eating hot, but that is purely one of preference. Heat the oven to 375°F (190°C). Rub the fish all over with olive oil and salt and pepper. Lay the fish on a large sheet of foil. Into the cavity insert a sliced lemon and several stalks of leaf fennel. If you don't have any fennel, use a few drops of Pernod. You can also use melissa or lemon verbena, which is a good way of disposing of these over prolific plants. Wrap the fish in the foil and cook in the preheated oven 10 minutes per pound (500g.). Unwrap, skin, transfer to a platter, and serve with Hollandaise Sauce (see page 146).

smoked salmon

gravadlax

I grew up in St. John's Wood, London, which at that time was a predominantly Jewish area. My parents were both to a greater or lesser degree expatriate Scots, so I learned very early the difference between the London and the Scottish smoke. The Scots have given to the world the gift of cold-smoked fish; all other cultures smoke it hot or preserve it in some other way. Indeed in 1861, when kippers were first smoked at Crastair, the record reads "smoked in the way that Scots smoke salmon." The Scottish smoke is a much darker, deeper smoke. The fish is marinated usually in whiskey and brown sugar before smoking and comes out a deep orangy-pinky colour. It is nice to imagine that the Scots traders who went to Russia introduced the Russians to the idea and certainly what is now known as "London smoke" came to England with the Russian Jewish immigrants off the onion boats in the 1890s. The smoked salmon trade in London was dominated by the Jewish community when I was young, and for all I know is still. The London smoke is a paler, oilier variety, very delicate against the robust Scots version.

A plate of smoked salmon is to my mind a perfect appetizer, and all it needs is a little lemon juice and both black and cayenne pepper. There is a growing fashion to serve it in the Russian manner with chopped onions and hard-boiled eggs, but I only like this in New York, where the best of breakfasts is smoked salmon with chopped onion, capers, cream cheese, and a bagel. This is another fashion brought to America by the Russian Jews, and only in New York can you find the perfect bagel.

Choose the smoke you like and the supplier you like. Even some supermarkets sell quite good smoked salmon, but remember to be lavish with it or don't serve it at all.

The name means "buried" or "grave" salmon in Norse, because originally the fish was buried in the permafrost. My friend, the photographer Karin Simon, is acclaimed throughout London's Swedish community as the doyenne of gravadlax, and this is her recipe together with her recipe for Dill Sauce (see page 145). The freezing part is designed to kill any bugs and certainly doesn't hurt the flavour of the dish.

Serves 4–6

2 fillets of raw salmon, about $^3/4$ pound (350g.) each, with skin left on
2 tablespoons each per small fillet of equal measures of mixed salt and superfine sugar
freshly ground white pepper
a large bunch of dill (keep the dill tips for the sauce and use the rest for the gravadlax)

Take a shallow dish large enough to hold the fillets flat (if you don't have this, you can put them in a plastic bag without holes to keep the liquid in). Sprinkle the fillets with some of the salt and sugar mixture. Put some of the mixture into the bottom of the dish and place a fillet skin-side down on top of it. Generously cover the salted sugared flesh with dill and place the other fillet on top, skin-side up. Sprinkle with the rest of the salt and sugar and the pepper, then place a board or plate over this, and weigh the whole thing down.

Put the dish in the refrigerator inside a plastic bag and turn it all every 2 hours, keeping the skin sides out. Leave for 48–60 hours, then transfer to the freezer, and freeze for a day.

Defrost well, carve, and serve with Dill Sauce (see page 145).

carving fish

smoked salmon

Some years ago, while poking about in the attic, I came upon a flat, oblong, leather-covered box. Inside I discovered a fish trowel and matching fork with ivory handles and silver-gilt metalwork of quite hideous mid-Victorian design. They were covered in elaborate scrollwork of a distinctly funereal pattern, and even the ivory handles, which the Georgians would have left gracefully alone, had been heavily carved and decorated at their ends with what appeared to be pineapples. Engraved on the blade of the fish trowel is "Presented to Mr Joseph Scott by the household staff of Trimdon Grange on the occasion of his majority. Nov. 21st 1862". Seated among the dust and cobwebs, leather-bound traveling cases, japanned deed boxes and old hunting boots, I had a vision of the scheming that must have gone on in the butler's pantry as the senior domestic staff plotted to outdo their rivals on the estate staff. And finally decided on this set of ghastly utensils which, after their solemn presentation, had obviously remained unused in their case for over a hundred years.

I am glad I decided not to put them back where I found them, because they have proved incredibly useful over the years. With a bit of mayonnaise smeared over the blades, they don't look too frightful...

There was a period in my life, albeit a pretty brief one, when I did a stint in the City. This was intended to broaden my education and give me some sort of commercial acumen which, it was hoped, would be of future benefit to my career as a farmer. The tedium of life as a junior aviation broker was relieved every lunchtime when I escaped from the Lloyd's building and hurried to nearby Leadenhall Market. Here, among the stalls selling fish and seafood, sides of beef and lamb, bundles of chickens, ducks, geese, and, in the winter, pheasants, partridges, and hares, I felt slightly more at home. At one of the stalls, a group of three ancient men stood all day deftly slicing sides of the finest smoked salmon. If I felt there was no pressing need for me to return to the Room, I would stand for ages watching the hypnotic ease with which these old men in their white coats reduced their individual smoked salmons to a pile of glistening, delectable, orange slices.

Everyone loves smoked salmon. As an appetizer, good smoked salmon is hard to beat, and the best way to spoil your guests is to slice it yourself, a prospect most people find beyond contemplation. This is a pity, because with the right knife and a bit of courage, you can take the quantum leap, from the very recognizable prepacked slices or even those done by a professional, to that half of smoked salmon on the sideboard that one has obviously sliced oneself.

The knife is all-important. It needs to be flexible but short enough to retain a degree of rigidity, with a straight, round-ended blade 1 inch (2.5cm.) wide and 10 inches (25cm.) long. A side of smoked salmon will be slightly concave in the middle, and slicing is against the grain—that is, from the tail toward the head—and starts a third of the way down the

gravadlax

body. A tip I learned from watching the old men in Leadenhall Market is to wipe the blade with olive oil before you start and periodically thereafter. This helps the knife to run through the flesh more smoothly. More than anything else, the knife must be very sharp.

Hold the knife at an angle of 5 degrees and, keeping it at that angle, take off the first slice, $1/12$ inch (2mm.) thick. This and the next two or three will be fairly narrow, but will very quickly become wider. It is essential that the angle is maintained as you proceed down the length of the fish to insure slices that are as large as possible. Always use the whole length of the knife blade, wipe frequently with olive oil, and let the knife do the work. Do not, at any time, try to force the knife through. Above all, give it a try. It's fun to do and your guests are not likely to mind if the slices are not exactly uniform in size or thickness.

For those lucky enough to acquire a whole side of salmon cured in the Scandinavian fashion, the carving principle is the same as for smoked salmon, but the slices can afford to be slightly thicker, up to $1/8$ inch (3mm.) thick.

To slice gravadlax, I suggest using a knife with a wavy edge, designed to avoid clogging with fat, rather than one with a straight edge rubbed in olive oil.

Slice at an angle of 5 degrees, $1/12$ inch (2mm.) thick for smoked salmon and $1/8$ inch (3mm.) for gravadlax.

1. Run the blade of the fish trowel down the backbone. Select a 3 inch (7.5cm.) section, slice over ribs and remove.

2 Continue down one side and then the other.

hot or cold poached salmon, sea trout, or cod

The sight of these fish laid out in all their glory, glistening with aspic and decorated with cucumber slices at a buffet lunch, throws people into a complete dither, unless someone is on hand to serve them. Most will move smartly on to the sliced ham or chicken. But serving the flesh of a large fish is actually the least onerous of all jobs, and very easy.

The salmon, sea trout, or cod will arrive from the kitchen, lying on its side with the skin removed and the spine easily identifiable, once the decorations have been removed, by the join in the flesh pattern. Simply run the blade of the fish trowel down this division from head to tail, pressing slightly from side to side to ease the flesh. Starting at the head, where the flesh is thickest and on the side opposite the belly, insert your trowel about 3 inches (7.5cm.) down and at right angles to the spine, and cut through until it is clear. Use your fish fork at the same time so that, as the flesh comes away, you ease it onto the blade of the trowel to transport the section of fish to a nearby plate. Increase the size of section as you move towards the tail and the body of the fish becomes narrower.

When the flesh is cleared down to the tail, start again at the head, lifting the sections down towards the belly side, and repeat until the backbone is completely exposed. Putting aside your trowel and fork, lift the tail between forefinger and thumb. The backbone and head will come free, leaving the remaining fillet to be cut into sections and served.

3 When the flesh is cleared from one side, lift the backbone out by the tail.

turbot

choosing and cooking turbot

Turbot is an expensive fish but truly wonderful. You should be able to get hold of turbot in a good fish store, but the large fish of my youth are no longer available. The most common purchase will be of a chicken turbot, a young fish of about 2 1/4– 2 3/4 pounds (1–1.3kg.) that you can cook whole in the oven and skin before serving. Fillets are usually cut from the smaller fish, and are rather disappointing, but cutlets will come from larger fish and are better value. If your fish store has a large fish, ask for a piece for this dish because the more mature the fish, the better the flavor. (In Scotland turbot is called "bannock fluke" because its body is as round as a bannock or oatcake.)

turbot with warm tomato vinaigrette

This is an excellent way of cooking turbot, and the tomato vinaigrette makes an unusual accompaniment. You can also make this recipe with halibut or hake, which are cheaper. The trick with nonoily fish is never to let any liquid near them until they are cooked, using only oil or butter. Cold turbot is wonderful with a green herb sauce (see page 145).

Serves 4-6

1 chicken turbot or piece of turbot, about 2 1/4–2 3/4 pounds (1–1.3kg.)
6 large sprigs of rosemary
salt and freshly ground black pepper
2 tablespoons olive oil
1/4 stick (25g.) butter

Sauce
10 tablespoons olive oil
4 teaspoons white wine vinegar
2 tablespoons finely chopped tomatoes

Heat the oven to 350°F (180°C).

Place the rosemary in a roasting pan and lay the turbot on top. Season, then pour over the oil and dab on the butter. Roast in the oven 35–40 minutes.

For the sauce, heat the oil and vinegar together in a small pan, then add the tomatoes and some salt and pepper. Warm through and serve with the fish.

1 The whole turbot.

2 Scrape away the little bones that surround the fish.

carving turbot

Turbot is one of the largest flat fishes. To serve a whole one, first scrape away the little bones attached to the end of the ribs that surround the fish. With these cleared away, proceed as for salmon, sea trout, or cod (see pages 122–123). Slice along the backbone and free the flesh around the gills. Select a suitable portion, depending on the size of the fish, then slice down from the spine over the ribs and lift free.

3 Run the trowel down the fish backbone; select a suitable-sized portion and lift free.

sauces, vegetables, and accompaniments

savory condiments and sauces: general

stock

It is a good idea to make stock from the bones and carcasses of your cooking activities, and then to reduce it right down. Pour it into an ice cube tray, freeze it, and store the cubes until needed, when they can be melted and more water added to bring them up to the desired strength.

To your bones or carcass add water and onion, leek, celery, or carrot. Bring the stock to a boil and simmer uncovered at least 1 hour, skimming during this time. If you have an Aga, the bottom oven makes excellent stock, but bring it to a boil on the top first. At the end it will have reduced by about one third. Strain the stock and leave it to get cold, then remove the fat. At this stage reduce it for your ice cube tray. Out of the freezer, stock will keep for a week in the refrigerator, but boil it up again after two days.

You can also make fish stock, but don't do this with oily fish because it is horrid.

Stock is useful for both sauces and soups, and a kind butcher may give you or sell you cheaply a bone or two to add to your carcass. Boil up your giblets to make stock if they come with the bird.

gravy

Pour off the fat in the bottom of the roasting pan, and scrape up any bits of meat to enhance the sauce. Put in 1 tablespoon all-purpose flour, stir well to take up the juices, then allow to cook a minute or two. Pour on some stock, some vegetable cooking water, wine or beer, or any combination of these, stirring as you go. When you have reached the desired thickness, adjust the seasoning and strain into a gravy boat. Don't, if you are inviting me to dinner, use gravy granules or stock cubes: It is a waste of money unless you have an addiction to the flavor.

An Argyle gravy boat which pours from below the surface to remove any lingering fat is a good idea, or you can add a little brandy and set fire to the gravy in the pan to minimize grease.

white sauce

for beef

horseradish sauce

Every girl of my generation was taught the basic white sauce, which is invaluable for so many things. White sauce is the basis of a soufflé; with fish stock and truffles it is Sauce Cardinal; with crayfish butter, Sauce Nantua; with cream, Sauce Crème; and with onion, Sauce Soubise. More simply, if you add parsley, it's a parsley sauce, cheese and it's a cheese sauce (or Sauce Mornay), and if you change the milk to stock, you have a Velouté Sauce.

Makes about 1¼ cups (300ml.)

¼ stick (25g.) butter
2 tablespoons plain flour
2½ cups (600ml.) milk
salt and freshly ground black pepper

Melt the butter in a heavy pan and toss in the flour. Stir vigorously with a wooden spoon until it is mixed to a paste, then cook over a low heat 2–3 minutes, still stirring. Pour in a third of the milk and allow it to heat through before stirring it to mix. Continue until all the milk is used up. Season and simmer until cooked and reduced to the desired consistency.

The classic accompaniment for beef, horseradish was once revered as a famous antiscorbutic, and is still a great asset with other fattier meats such as goose or pork for aiding digestion. It is to my mind underused, and you will find it cropping up in the leftovers section. Horseradish is easy to grow (too easy in fact) and should be contained in a bucket to prevent it taking over the entire vegetable garden. It can be found in wild places, and is usually a mark of monastic habitation. You can occasionally find it fresh in Asian stores or farmers' markets if you don't grow your own.

It is best to grate it in a processor to save both fingers and eyes. Lean back when you take the lid off, or you will stream. My mother said to grate horseradish was the best cure for colds. I tend to make the sauce entirely in a food processor. Both the made sauce and the grated root will store in a sealed jar, but the latter will lose strength with time.

Makes about 1¼ cups (300ml.)

1 horseradish root
⅔ cup (150ml.) heavy cream
1 teaspoon white wine vinegar
salt and freshly ground black pepper

Peel the root with a sharp knife. Grate it in the processor. Change the blade, add the other ingredients and mix well.

balkan horseradish sauce

This Balkan variant is best with boiled beef, and is very good with ham.

Makes about 1 cup (225ml.)

2 ounces (50g.) fresh horseradish, grated
4 tablespoons sour cream
salt
1 teaspoon superfine sugar
2 tablespoons white wine vinegar or lemon juice
1 hard-boiled egg yolk

Mix the horseradish and the cream, then add salt to taste along with the sugar and vinegar or lemon juice. Press the egg yolk through a strainer and mix it in well.

béarnaise sauce

Whether the good burghers of Béarn actually invented this sauce, or whether it was named in their honor, is lost in the mists of time, but it is wonderful with beef.

Makes about 1 cup (225ml.)

1¹/4 cups (300ml.) dry white wine
4 tablespoons white wine vinegar
2 shallots, finely chopped
4 tablespoons (15g.) each chopped tarragon and chervil
3 egg yolks
2 sticks (225g.) butter, diced
lemon juice (optional)

Reserving about 1 teaspoon of the chopped tarragon and chervil mixed, put the rest in a pan with the wine, vinegar, and shallots and boil until 2 tablespoons of liquid remain. Strain the reduction, and allow to cool slightly. Add the egg yolks, and place in a bowl over a pan of water that is gently simmering. Beat until the mixture thickens slightly, then add the butter dice gradually, stirring. Thin with lemon juice if necessary, and add the reserved chopped herbs.

for lamb

mint sauce

gooseberry mint sauce

In English food this is perhaps the last great survivor of the influence of the Crusades. There is no doubt that the idea of mint with lamb was brought back from the Levant, as were many other such recipes now defunct, but the rather curious, wet, and sharp mint sauce remains beloved of English cuisine.

Makes about 1/3 cup (85ml.)

a large handful of mint leaves, about 50
1 teaspoon superfine sugar
1 tablespoon boiling water
1 tablespoon white wine vinegar or lemon juice

Pound the mint leaves in a pestle and mortar. Cover with the sugar, and leave it to soak up the mint juice. Add just enough boiling water to dissolve the sugar and then add the vinegar or lemon juice to suit your taste. This will keep quite well in a tightly sealed jar in a cool place.   .

A tangy Regency variant on mint sauce uses gooseberries, which I find lifts the sauce.

Makes about 3/4 cup (200ml.)

6–8 ounces (175–225g.) gooseberries, topped and tailed
2 tablespoons water
1 tablespoon (15g.) butter
a pinch of superfine sugar
salt and freshly ground black pepper
1 tablespoon finely chopped mint leaves

Put the gooseberries in a pan with all the other ingredients except the mint. Bring to a boil and simmer 15–20 minutes until the fruit is tender. Purée in a blender, or push through a strainer. Stir in the mint leaves, leave to stand 2–3 minutes, and serve.

onion sauce

caper sauce

You can simply boil up onions with milk and seasoning, then strain them and use to make a roux-based white sauce with added cream, but this recipe from Lady Clarke of Tillypronie is slightly unusual and delicious.

Makes about 2^1/$_2$ cups (600ml.)

12 small onions, peeled
2^1/$_2$ cups (600ml.) water
salt and freshly ground black pepper
^{1}/$_2$ cup (25ml.) heavy cream

Boil the peeled onions in the water with a little salt until tender, then pass them through a strainer (or blend them). In a pan, heat the onion purée through with the cream and some more seasoning.

This sauce is best with boiled mutton, but is also good with lamb or salmon. It's pure Regency to me, harking back to an era when every kitchen had a barrel of these pickled flower buds of the caper plant. In England an alternative was pickled nasturtium buds, which are also good, but you'll have to pickle them yourself. Personally I use twice as many capers, but then I love capers...

Makes about ^{1}/$_2$ cup (125ml.)

^{1}/$_4$ stick (25g.) butter
1 tablespoon all-purpose flour
^{2}/$_3$ cup (150ml.) stock, heated
salt and freshly ground black pepper
1 egg yolk
2 tablespoons light cream
1 heaped tablespoons capers, chopped
^{1}/$_2$ tablespoon chopped parsley

In a small pan make a roux with half the butter and the flour, and cook for a few minutes, stirring. Moisten with a little of the hot stock and then keep mixing and adding the remaining stock until it is the consistency of thin cream. Season, and mix in the remaining butter. Beat the egg yolk with the cream and add to the sauce. Stir until it thickens, then add the capers with the parsley at the last minute.

for pork

apple sauce

It was a historical habit to serve animals with a sauce made from foods they themselves fed on. Orchard pigs were particularly favored for roasting: Indeed the Gloucester Old Spot was alleged to have developed its spots from the bruising caused by apples landing on its back!

Makes about 2/3 cup (150ml.)

3 cooking apples, peeled, cored, and chopped
1 onion, chopped
salt and freshly ground pepper
a knob of butter

Cook all the ingredients together with a little water until the apples collapse. Strain if liked, and serve.

luxury apple sauce

This curious recipe came from an old book on fruit cooking, *The Fruit Book*, by Paul Dinnage. It is very good.

Makes about 1¼ cups (300ml.)

3 apples, peeled, cored, and sliced
6 almonds, blanched and sautéed in a little butter
1 onion, chopped
grated zest of 1 orange
1 slice of white bread, toasted and dipped in
  white wine vinegar
freshly ground black pepper
1 teaspoon ground mixed spice
3 tablespoons each white wine and white wine vinegar

Put the apple slices, almonds, onion, orange zest, and bread in a saucepan. Season with the pepper and spice. Moisten with the wine and vinegar and cook until the apples are soft, about 15 minutes. Strain and serve hot.

apple sauce with madeira

An unusual French variant created in 1877 for the Duke of Dino by his chef Bichot. It is also good with game.

Makes about 1¼ cups (350ml.)

1¼ cups (300ml.) Madeira
juice and finely grated zest of 2 oranges
¾ cup (200ml.) apple purée
juice of 1 lemon

Put the Madeira and orange zest in a pan and boil to reduce by half. Add the apple purée and stir over a gentle heat to the desired thickness. Cool slightly, then add the orange and lemon juices.

prune sauce

This is a German sauce, *Zwetschgensaus*, which is very good with pork or goose.

Makes about 2 cups (450ml.)

⅓ cup (225g.) prunes, soaked overnight and drained
1 tablespoon (15g.) butter
1 tablespoon all-purpose flour
grated zest and juice of ½ lemon
1 tablespoon rum
a pinch of ground cinnamon
salt

Cover the prunes with water and cook 10 minutes or until soft. Drain and reserve the liquid. Pit and finely chop the prunes.

Melt the butter in a pan and make a roux with the flour. Cook for a minute, but do not brown. Stir in 1¼ cups (300ml.) liquid from the prunes, along with the lemon zest, rum, and cinnamon. Add the prunes, bring to a boil, stirring, and season with the lemon juice and salt.

for tongue

red wine sauce with raisins

This is a full, fruity sauce which goes well with tongue, but is also good with spiced beef, pork, or ham. It will keep well in the refrigerator for quite a long time, maturing as it goes.

Makes about 2$\frac{1}{2}$ cups (600ml.)

$\frac{1}{2}$ stick (50g.) butter
$\frac{3}{4}$ cup (75g.) all-purpose flour
$\frac{3}{4}$ cup (200ml.) stock
$\frac{3}{4}$ cup (200ml.) red wine
$\frac{1}{2}$ cup (75g.) raisins
1 strip of lemon zest
1 blade of mace
2 cloves
red wine vinegar or superfine sugar to taste (optional)

In a small pan make a roux with the butter and flour, and cook, stirring, until it turns dark yellow. Stir in the stock and then the wine. Add all the remaining ingredients except the vinegar or sugar and simmer 10 minutes or until the raisins have swelled up, stirring occasionally. Remove the lemon zest and spices and adjust the seasoning with a little wine vinegar or sugar depending on its tartness or lack of it.

for ham

cumberland sauce

This sauce is said to be named after Ernest, Duke of Cumberland, the brother of George IV and a well-known trencherman. Traditionally it is served with ham, but it is also very good with venison, tongue, or corned beef.

Makes about $\frac{3}{4}$ cup (200ml.)

zest and juice of 1 lemon
zest and juice of 1 orange
2 shallots, finely chopped
2 tablespoons redcurrant jelly
$\frac{2}{3}$ cup (150ml.) port
1 tablespoon white wine vinegar
a pinch of ground ginger
salt and cayenne pepper

Cut the orange and lemon zests into thin julienne strips, blanch in boiling water 1 minute, and drain. Blanch the shallots 2 minutes.

Heat the redcurrant jelly in a double saucepan or bain-marie, then add the citrus zests, shallots, port, vinegar, ginger, and orange and lemon juices. Season with salt and cayenne pepper to taste.

parsley sauce

This is basically a white sauce, with lots of parsley and a little mustard added.

Makes about 1¼ cups (300ml.)

2½ cups (600ml.) milk
a large bunch of curly parsley, chopped
½ stick (50g.) butter
½ cup (50g.) all-purpose flour
a pinch of English mustard powder
salt and freshly ground black pepper

Heat the milk and infuse half the parsley in it 2 minutes, then strain.

In a small pan make a roux with the butter and flour, then stir in the mustard powder and seasoning. Use the strained parsley milk to make the sauce, stirring in gently in the usual way (see page 130). Add the rest of the parsley and heat through.

mustard sauce

Another great traditional sauce, as often eaten with beef as ham. Johnny, a true Brit, eats mustard with most things... Until steel grinders were invented in the Industrial Revolution, the English boiled mustard seeds to make mustard sauce. In fact, the first ground mustard was presented to George III in Swaffham (Norfolk, where most English mustard is still grown), in the late eighteenth century.

Makes about 1 cup (225ml.)

2 sprigs each of parsley, tarragon, chives, chervil,
**   and salad burnet (or as available)**
4 hard-boiled egg yolks
4 tablespoons English mustard
4 tablespoons white wine vinegar
8 tablespoons olive oil

Blanch the herbs in boiling water, drain, and refresh in cold water. Place in a mortar and pound with the egg yolks. Transfer to a bowl, add the mustard and vinegar, and then slowly drizzle in the oil, stirring all the time as for mayonnaise.

for poultry and feathered game

bread sauce

A great many of you will have your own method of making this most ancient of sauces. The idea of using stale bread in sauces can be found in recipes dating back to the twelfth century, and there are various different types.

The most difficult problem with bread sauce is not to let it burn, and hence I always make mine in a double boiler. I buy double boilers whenever I see them in junk shops because they are the most useful of saucepans, but modern versions and inserts are not difficult to find.. Bread sauce can be made in advance and heated up or kept in the warming drawer until the bird is cooked, but a double boiler is much simpler. Try to use proper baked bread rather than the partly steamed stuff.

Makes about 2 cups (450ml.)

1 onion, liberally stuck with cloves
1 loaf of stale white bread, crust removed, cut into cubes
2¼ cups (600ml.) full-fat milk
a pinch of ground mace or freshly grated nutmeg
1 bay leaf
salt and freshly ground white pepper
⅔ cup (150ml.) heavy cream

Place the onion in a pan and arrange the bread haphazardly around it. Pour on the milk, and add the mace or nutmeg and the bay leaf. Bring to a boil and turn down to a very low heat, preferably with a heatproof mat under the pan.

Season and leave to simmer gently 2–3 hours, adding more milk if needed. The thickness of the sauce is purely one of preference. Just before serving, stir in the cream and heat through. Some people leave the onion in. Some remove the cloves, take the onion out, chop it finely, and return it to the sauce.

Cold bread sauce is great in sandwiches.

The idea of bread as a thickener for sauce is one that is as old as leavened bread. I like to think that the fact that the Romanians have this version is some indication that bread sauce was a Roman dish which the settled legions in this part of the world retained.

Romanian Bread Sauce

Makes about 2 cups (450ml.)

2 rolls, crumbled
2 garlic cloves, crushed
⅓ cup (90ml.) vegetable oil
1 cup (225ml.) stock
salt and freshly ground black pepper

Soak the crumbled rolls in water and squeeze well. Fry the garlic lightly in the oil in a pan and add the bread. Pour on the stock, season, and boil 5 minutes until thick.

red currant jelly or rowan jelly

I was sitting trying to remember the measurements when my friend Maggie rang. She makes jams for Scotland, and immediately said, "Don't be silly, darling, it's a pound of caster (superfine) sugar to a pint of juice". I once made 80 pounds (36kg.) of berries into jelly, which rather cured me, so I suck up to friends like Maggie... Rowan berries are the fruit of the mountain ash. You will have to pick your own as even in Scotland they aren't sold commercially.

Wash all your red currants or rowan berries on their stalks, then put into a heavy pan with enough water just to cover. Cook gently until the berries are just cooked. Turn into a jelly bag suspended over a large bowl and leave to drip overnight. Measure the juice, then bring to a boil with the appropriate amount of sugar, skimming occasionally. Boil until seething point is reached (when a spoonful on a cold saucer wrinkles as pushed). Cool a little, then put into jars, and store.

If you press the pulp to get more from it, your jelly will be cloudy and the increase won't be that great.

cranberry sauce

What the Americans eat with their Thanksgiving turkey, we Brits don't, but it's still a good sauce!

Makes about 2¹/₂ cups (600ml.)

2¹/₄ pounds (1kg.) cranberries
2²/₃ cups (500g.) superfine sugar
1²/₃ cups (400ml.) water

Pick over the cranberries and wash if necessary. Combine the sugar with the water in a pan and bring this to a boil. Simmer 10 minutes, then add the cranberries. Cover and cook until they stop popping. Skim the froth and cool before serving. You can add a dash of brandy if you like.

bosnian cranberry sauce

The hills of Europe are all full of berries, and cranberries grow wild in Bosnia—or did before the war. Still, the cranberry is a hardy plant, so they are probably still making this variant on the sauce.

Makes about 2 cups (500ml.)

1 pound (500g.) cranberries
2/3 cup (150ml.) water
2 tablespoons capers, chopped
2 tablespoons English mustard powder

Cook the cranberries in the water 20–25 minutes until very tender, then strain or blend them and allow to cool. Add the capers. Dilute the mustard with a small amount of the purée, then mix it all in well.

sauce bigarade

This is the classic sauce for wild duck, and *bigarade* in French means a wild orange. Seville oranges are available in the U.K, but in the U.S.A. bitter oranges may be hard to find.

Makes about 2¹/₂ cups (600ml.)

2 Seville oranges
juice of 1 lemon
2¹/₂ cups (600ml.)
Velouté Sauce (see page 130)

Pare the zest from the oranges and cut it into julienne strips. Parboil the strips in water 3 minutes, drain, and dry. Squeeze the juice from the oranges. Mix the orange and lemon juices into the Velouté Sauce, strain, and add the strips of orange zest.

sauce celia

This is an interesting "white sauce" given by Mrs. Rundell in her early nineteenth-century cooking tome, and its name and origins led to much discussion between our editor, Susan Fleming, and myself. I decided to rename it after another editor, our managing editor, the redoubtable Celia Kent. She has been a tower of strength throughout this book and the last, and she deserves a cheer of recognition, not least because, when accompanying us during the making of the television series *Clarissa and the Countryman*, she received a clout across the head from an anti...

Makes about 3 cups (750ml.)

1¹/₄ cups (300ml.) chicken stock
1 large blade of mace
2 cloves
15 peppercorns
4 salted anchovies, rinsed and finely chopped
1 stick (100g.) butter, kneaded with 1 tablespoon flour
1¹/₄ cups (300ml.) heavy cream

Boil the stock in a pan with the mace, cloves, and peppercorns about 10 minutes.

Strain into a saucepan and add the anchovies and butter-and-flour. Add the cream and simmer briskly 2 minutes, stirring continuously.

tarragon sauce

A slightly complicated version from the Troisgros brothers, the alleged founders of "nouvelle cuisine."

Makes about $3/4$ cup (200ml.)

5 ounces (150g.) spinach leaves, trimmed
$1/4$ stick (25g.) butter
$3/4$ cup (200ml.) chicken stock
1 cup (50g.) tarragon leaves
30 white peppercorns, crushed
salt

Wash the spinach leaves and cook a few minutes with the butter until they wilt.

In a separate pan, bring the stock to a boil. Using a strainer, dip the tarragon leaves into it, and refresh in cold water. Return the tarragon to the stock, add the peppercorns, and boil rapidly until the liquid has virtually evaporated (about 15 minutes). Add the spinach and salt to taste, and heat through. Purée in a blender or pass through a strainer.

lady muriel beckwith's sauce for wild duck

The Beckwiths are the family of the Marquis of Hedford. This was a recipe that was given to my mother by the present Marquis who used to pop around to our house to have his white tie tied by my sisters.

Makes about $1/2$ cup (125ml.)

juice of 1 lemon
2 teaspoons English mustard
salt and freshly ground black pepper
cayenne pepper
2 tablespoons port
6 tablespoons poultry stock

Mix the lemon juice, mustard and some salt together in a small pan. Add black pepper and cayenne pepper as liked. Pour in the port and stock, mix until smooth, heat, and serve.

oyster sauce

Traditionally eaten with turkey in eighteenth-century England and in the U.S.A.. A number of recipes from this period exist where the turkey is stuffed with oysters, but I find this too much...

Makes about $1^2/_3$ cups (450ml.)

2–3 dozen oysters
$^3/_4$ cup (200ml.) dry white wine
1 shallot, finely chopped
$^1/_2$ stick (50g.) butter
1 tablespoon all-purpose flour
freshly ground black pepper
freshly grated nutmeg
2 egg yolks
juice of 1 lemon

Open the oysters and drain the liquor into a pan. Place this over the heat and add half the white wine. When the liquor comes to a boil, add the oysters, simmer 2 minutes, then drain, and trim.

In a separate pan, fry the shallot in half the butter without browning. Sprinkle in the flour and stir to make a roux. Stir in the rest of the wine and 1 cup (25ml.) oyster liquor. Add some pepper and a dash of nutmeg.

Leave to cook gently until it coats the back of a spoon. Beat together the egg yolks and lemon juice, and stir in a few spoonfuls of sauce. Return to the pan of sauce, and gently heat through until it thickens, stirring. Whisk in the remaining butter. Add the oysters, heat through, and serve.

for fish

sorrel sauce

I love the fresh sharp spring taste of sorrel, a well-known antiscorbutic. As someone who has had scurvy, boy, can you feel it doing you good!

Makes about ³/₄ cup (200ml.)

¹/₂ cup (100ml.) fish stock
¹/₂ cup (100ml.) dry white wine
2 shallots, chopped
¹/₂ cup (125ml.) heavy cream
1 cup (50g.) sorrel, cut into strips
¹/₄ stick (25g.) butter, cut into small pieces
salt and freshly ground black pepper
lemon juice

Put the stock, wine, and shallots into a pan and heat until reduced to 1 tablespoon of syrupy liquid. Pour in the cream and bring to a boil. Remove from the heat and add the sorrel. Add the butter piece by piece, and melt by moving the pan around. Season with salt and pepper, and add lemon juice to taste.

mayonnaise

I know a family, all of whose female members can make perfect mayonnaise with a bowl and a fork, and I also know serious cooks who flunk it four times in ten. I like the richness of pure olive oil, but some people prefer to mix it with vegetable oil.

Makes about 2 cups (450ml.)

2 egg yolks
salt and freshly ground white pepper
2 cups (450ml.) oil of choice
juice of 1 lemon

Put the egg yolks into a generous bowl, and add a pinch of salt and a grind of pepper. Beat them with a fork or lightly whisk until they are pale yellow. Drip the olive oil in very carefully, beating constantly as you go, until the mixture begins to emulsify or thicken. Keep beating and adding oil until all the oil has been incorporated. If it becomes too thick, add a little lemon juice and possibly a little hot water.

If it splits, take another egg yolk and a few drops of lemon juice and add the failed mayonnaise to it spoonful by spoonful, whisking constantly.

languedoc green sauce

This sauce, which I like to think was eaten by Eleanor of Aquitaine, is excellent with game fish, but is also good with veal and pheasant.

Makes about 2 cups (500ml.)

2 garlic cloves
1 shallot
2 scallions
$1/2$ cup (25g.) watercress
3 sprigs of tarragon
2 sprigs of parsley
1 sprig of chervil
1 sprig of rosemary or thyme
2 cups (500ml.) white wine
1 cup (250ml.) white stock
1 tablespoon olive oil
salt and freshly ground black pepper

Finely chop the garlic, shallot, scallions, watercress, and all the herbs.

In a small saucepan, boil together the wine, stock, and olive oil until reduced to half their original volume. Turn down the heat and add all the chopped ingredients. Heat the sauce until it just comes to a boil, then season, and pour into a hot sauce boat.

dill sauce

The only accompaniment for gravadlax. The mustard used for this is Swedish, which is easily obtainable if you have an IKEA nearby; if not, use a mild Dijon mustard. Don't buy readymade dill sauce, because it is universally second rate. Use the dill tips left over from making Gravadlax (see page 118).

Makes about 1 cup (225ml.)

2 tablespoons Swedish mustard
1 tablespoon superfine sugar
1 tablespoon white wine vinegar
about $2/3$ cup (150ml.) good vegetable oil
dill tips, finely chopped (see above)

Mix the mustard, sugar, and vinegar and beat well together. You can use an electric beater. Pour in the oil gradually as for Mayonnaise (see page 144)—you may need more or less than stated above—and continue to beat until the sauce emulsifies or thickens. Store in the refrigerator and, just before serving, add the dill tips.

hollandaise

tomato sauce

I love hollandaise and will make it anywhere, even on a campsite with a cup and a bowl of hot water, although my friends will testify that I get so angry that it emulsifies from sheer brute force!

It can also be made in a microwave oven. You melt the butter first, whip it into the egg yolks and lemon juice, then cook at number five for 30 seconds. Remove the bowl from the microwave and beat the contents fiercely. Return to the microwave and cook for a further minute. Stir again, add a dash of cold water and serve.

Makes about 1^{1}/$_{4}$ cups (300ml.)

2 large egg yolks
1 tablespoon cold water
1 tablespoon lemon juice
salt and freshly ground white pepper
2 sticks (225g.) cold butter, cut in pieces

Use a doubleboiler or a bowl over boiling water. Place the yolks, water, lemon juice, salt, and pepper in the top saucepan and beat until the yolks are smooth. Add the butter piece by piece and, as the butter is absorbed, add more. The sauce will become thick and creamy. If it splits, add a dash of cold water and beat frantically.

This is a good, straightforward tomato sauce, which can be used in a variety of ways. It freezes well.

Makes about 2 cups (450ml.)

2^{1}/$_{4}$–2^{3}/$_{4}$ pounds (1–1.3kg.) ripe tomatoes, chopped
^{1}/$_{4}$ stick (25g.) butter
^{1}/$_{2}$ onion, thinly sliced
1 celery stalk, diced
1 tablespoon olive oil
1 teaspoon superfine sugar
^{1}/$_{2}$ teaspoon salt

Melt the butter in a pan and cook the onion and celery until softened. Add the tomatoes, oil, sugar, and salt and simmer 30 minutes, or until the sauce is thickened. Strain and use.

vegetables and accompaniments

fried breadcrumbs

It is one of the glories of a roast dinner that it lends itself splendidly to creative vegetables and accompaniments. With an intricate created dish, the vegetables tend to be perforce plain on the basis that you don't wish to detract from the complications of the main dish. Here the vegetables can be adventurous and still complementary. I haven't run through the whole vegetable world, just those that traditionally—or in my mind—especially favor a roast. The cabbage is of course essential for that most delicious of leftovers, Bubble and Squeak (see page 165), and we have to include that quintessential roast beef accompaniment, Yorkshire pudding.

I make a lot of these in season, so do trust me— I have the recipe down to a fine art.

Take a sandwich loaf of day-old white bread and remove the crumb from the crust. In a heavy skillet melt 2 sticks (175g.) butter and 2 tablespoons of olive oil. Add the bread, literally torn into pieces, and cook very slowly over a low heat, bashing the bread with a spatula as it starts to color. It will, with a little help, break down into breadcrumbs and take up the fat. If it looks like drying out, add a bit more oil. Cook gently about 30 minutes until the required brown in color. Leave in the pan and reheat before serving.

yorkshire pudding

I was invited recently to dine with the Butchers' Guild in York for their annual Shrove Tuesday Feast. It was a splendid affair, full of love of good food and laughter. On this occasion the Yorkshire pudding was served in the traditional manner as a course before the meat course with onion gravy. This was designed to fill you up and make you therefore less hungry for the beef so you would appreciate it more. I was told that it is also customary to save a slice to have later with jam, no doubt the origin of the American popover.

When I was young the Yorkshire pudding was baked in a roasting pan as a large slab. Today the fashion is for little individual puddings which are quicker and easier to make, but I still prefer the larger piece. The trick, apart from a good batter, is to have the dripping in the pan smoking hot before you pour in the batter.

Serves 6

1 cup (110g.) all-purpose flour
salt and freshly ground black pepper
2 eggs
1¼ cups (300ml.) milk
fat from the roasting pan, dripping, or vegetable oil

Sift the flour and some salt and pepper into a bowl and make a well in the middle. Break in the eggs and beat well together, gradually working in the flour. Beat in the milk, using a good wrist action to beat in air. Make sure the mixture is well mixed and free of lumps. Leave to stand at least 30 minutes.

Heat the oven to 425°F (220°C).

Heat the pan or muffin pans if making individual puddings. Put about 2 tablespoons of dripping in the large pan, 1 teaspoon in each of the smaller ones. Put in the oven until the fat smokes. Pour in the batter and bake 25–30 minutes.

If you don't have two ovens, you will have to recalculate your meat cooking time. This is not as difficult as it sounds because the meat will be out of the oven for 15 minutes' resting. You can reduce the overall cooking time by 10 minutes to allow for the higher end temperature: It will not hurt the meat at this stage.

pease pudding

pickled onions

What does the rhyme say? "Pease pudding hot, pease pudding cold, pease pudding in the pot, nine days old." Oh, I love pease pudding. In Durham it is still sold commercially and spread on "stottie bread" (bread cooked in the bottom of the oven) and good ham with the fat on. Whenever I cook a ham or a piece of pickled pork, I put a clothful of peas in to cook with it. I also freeze my ham stock so I can cook the peas in it.

Serves 6–8

2¹/₄ pounds (1kg.) split peas
2 egg yolks
¹/₄ stick (25g.) butter
salt and freshly ground black pepper

Soak the peas overnight in plenty of cold water. Tie the soaked and drained peas loosely in a cloth and boil in plenty of fresh water to cover (or ham stock or with a ham) about 1¹/₂ hours. Remove from the pan and untie, then rub the peas through a strainer or mouli. Dry the peas in a pan over a gentle heat until thick, then stir in the butter, egg yolks, and salt and pepper to taste.

So much better if you do your own. If you like chili, choose one to suit your taste.

Makes 2¹/₄ pounds (1kg.)

2¹/₄ pounds (1kg.) small pickling onions
¹/₂ cup (125g.) salt
1 quart (1 liter) malt vinegar
²/₃ cup (125g.) sugar
25g pickling spice
10 cloves
10 black peppercorns
1 fresh red chili pepper

Put the onions in boiling water for a few minutes to soften their skins, then drain and peel. Cover with salt and leave 24 hours. In a pan, make an infusion of the vinegar, sugar, and spices, heating to melt the sugar. Add the onions and boil gently about 5 minutes. The onions should still be hard in the center. Pot and cover with the vinegar and spices. Add the chili which you have pricked all over. Seal and leave at least 2 weeks before use.

my chutney

There was a time when I made lots of chutney, and this is the recipe I used.

Makes about 5 pounds (2.5kg.)

2^1/$_4$ **pounds (1kg.) each green tomatoes, cooking apples, and onions, peeled (the apples cored as well) and chopped**
2 chilies, seeded and thinly sliced
^{3}/$_4$ **ounce (20g.) freshly grated nutmeg**
^{3}/$_4$ **cup (125g.) golden raisins**
1^2/$_3$ **cups (350g.) brown sugar**
2^1/$_2$ **cups (600ml.) malt vinegar**
3^1/$_2$ **tablespoons (75g.) clear honey**
3 tablespoons (20g.) ground cloves
^{3}/$_4$ **cup (125g.) raisins**
a pinch of cayenne pepper

Put the tomatoes, apples, and onions in a bowl, stir together, and leave covered in a cool place overnight. The next day put all the ingredients in a large pan, bring to a boil and cook gently 2 hours, stirring often. Put in jars and seal. I always use the vacuum-packed chestnuts you can buy ready-peeled in good gourmet stores.

chestnut stuffing

Makes about 2^1/$_4$ pounds (1kg.)

1^1/$_4$ **sticks (125g.) butter**
2 shallots, finely chopped
2^1/$_4$ **pounds (1kg.) chestnuts, peeled**
salt and freshly ground black pepper

Melt the butter in a pan and gently fry the shallots 2–3 minutes, then add the chestnuts, and cook until they begin to crumble, about 5 minutes. Season with salt and pepper, then mash slightly with a fork. Leave to cool before stuffing into the neck end of your turkey.

apricot and apple stuffing

Good with lamb or pork.

Makes 1 pound (500g.)

1/2 cup (75g.) dried apricots, soaked
2/3 cup (125g.) cooking apples, peeled and chopped
2/3 cup (75g.) shelled walnuts, finely chopped
finely grated zest of 1 lemon
2 1/2 cups (150g.) fresh white breadcrumbs
salt and freshly ground black pepper
3/4 stick (75g.) butter, melted

Chop the apricots finely and mix with all the other ingredients, binding with the melted butter.

fruit and mushroom stuffing

A very useful stuffing, good with anything.

Makes 1 1/3 pounds (600g.)

8 ounces (225g.) fresh redcurrants or redcurrant jelly
1 tablespoon water
2 tablespoons (25g.) superfine sugar
1/3 cup (50g.) onion, chopped
1/4 stick (25g.) butter
2/3 cup (50g.) mushrooms (stalks will do), chopped
1/4 pound (125g.) belly pork or fat bacon, minced
2/3 cup (25g.) parsley, chopped
3/4 cup (50g.) fresh white breadcrumbs
1/2 garlic clove, crushed
a pinch of thyme
salt and freshly ground black pepper
1 small egg

Cook the redcurrants or jelly with the water and sugar until soft, then strain if using the fruit. In a separate pan, cook the onion in the butter over a gentle heat until soft, then add the mushrooms, and cook for a little longer. In a bowl mix the onion/mushroom mixture with the pork or fat bacon, parsley, and breadcrumbs. Stir in the redcurrants and the garlic, thyme, and seasoning, and bind with the egg.

sausagemeat stuffing

oyster stuffing

Ask your butcher for well-flavored sausagemeat, or break up some of those fancy sausages: Sun-dried tomato ones are particularly good, or pork and leek.

Makes 2¼ pounds (1kg.)

2¼ pounds (1kg.) sausagemeat
2 shallots, finely chopped
salt and freshly ground black pepper

Mix all the ingredients together and stuff into the neck end of the bird.

Traditional with turkey but good with all white-meat birds, or with lamb.

Makes about ¾ pound (350g.)

12 oysters
2 cups (125g.) fresh white breadcrumbs
finely grated zest of ½ lemon
1 tablespoon chopped parsley
½ stick (50g.) butter, melted
salt and cayenne pepper
1 egg yolk

Remove the oysters from their shells and reserve the liquor. Chop the oysters. Mix the oysters with the breadcrumbs, lemon zest and parsley, stir in the melted butter and season with salt and cayenne. Bind the stuffing with the egg yolk and a little reserved oyster liquor.

potatoes

roast potatoes

After that, let us start with potatoes. The wonder of a perfect roast dinner is, of course, the roast potato. These are so popular that large commercial companies actually offer ready-cooked roast potatoes. Make sure to find a good roasting variety of potato, because waxy salad potatoes don't do well.

Roasting potatoes is not simply a matter of putting them around the roast. You can do this if your oven and roasting pan are large enough, but you will seldom get perfect roast potatoes. There are two very important things to remember about roast potatoes. The first is that the fat they go into must be searing hot. The second is that they must have drained properly and stopped steaming completely after their parboiling. If you fail on either of these two counts, you will have soggy roast potatoes.

The next consideration is the fat that you roast them in. Without a moment's hesitation I will tell you that the most perfect medium is goose fat. If you are a cholesterol freak, I would point out that the lowest incidence of heart problems is found in the goose region of France... Of the other fats, lard and dripping are better than oil, but if you wish to use oil, use vegetable not olive.

Peel your potatoes and half or quarter them. Allow three pieces of potato per person. Put them into a large pan of cold water, add salt, and bring to a boil. Boil 5 minutes, then drain into a colander at once. Leave until all the steam has evaporated, which will take 20 minutes or more.

Put an extra roasting pan on top of the stove and put in your fat. When melted this should be the depth of the first digit of your middle finger. Heat the fat until it is smoking, then put your potatoes into it carefully without removing from the heat. Open the oven and put the pan in with the roast, but above it, and roast 1 hour. Calculate it so that they come to the table straight at the end of their cooking time. About 15 minutes before the end of cooking, strain off the surplus fat. Drain the potatoes well on paper towels.

seethed potatoes

May Byron was a pre-First World War cook who produced a great many books on useful things like vegetable cooking and puddings. This recipe is very good with salmon or white meat at a time when there aren't fresh new potatoes. The redoubtable Mrs. Byron says of this method, "No one who has not eaten potatoes thus prepared can conceive how delicious they are."

Serves 2–4

1 pound (500g.) small potatoes, scrubbed
salt
1/4 stick (25g.) butter

Put the potatoes in a Dutch oven with a sprinkling of salt, the butter, and very little water. Cook uncovered over a very low heat 40 minutes, or until tender.

potatoes with mustard seeds

A dish adapted from one in *The Compleat Mustard* by Robin Weir and Rosamund Mann, which is excellent with cold meat or roast chicken.

Serves 2–4

1 pound (500g.) large new potatoes, scrubbed
sea salt
1^1/$_2$ tablespoons groundnut oil
1 medium onion, finely chopped
1 small garlic clove
1/2 teaspoon Dijon mustard
2 tablespoons brown mustard seeds
1 small bunch of cilantro, finely chopped (or use parsley instead)

Boil the potatoes in salted water until nearly tender, then drain and slice thickly.

Heat the oil in a large pan and fry the onion until softened and golden. Crush the garlic with a pinch of salt and mix with the mustard. Add this to the pan and cook another 2 minutes to crisp the onion and release the aroma of the garlic. Push to the sides of the pan and fry the mustard seeds until they start to pop. Add the potatoes and stir gently so as not to break them up. Cook until the potatoes are lightly browned, then transfer to a serving dish, and sprinkle with chopped cilantro.

game chips

The secret of good game chips lies in slicing the potatoes very thinly (use a mandolin), soaking all the starch out, drying them properly, and cooking them in lard or beef dripping which will hold a high enough temperature otherwise they go soggy. You need a deep-fat fryer so you can cook them at the last minute.

Serves 4

1 pound (450g.) old potatoes
1 cup (250g.) lard or beef dripping

Peel and slice the potatoes as thinly as possible. Put them in very cold water to soak for 10 minutes, then remove them, pat dry with a towel and transfer to another towel to dry properly. Heat the fat until it is smoking and fry the chips in small batches, draining on to kitchen paper in a warm bowl. Serve at once.

pommes clarise

This simple method of cooking potatoes was so dubbed by my nephew Edward. It is the simplest of gratins and you can of course make gratins with anything that takes your fancy, using stock, bacon, cream, and tomatoes— the experimentation will give you hours of fun!

Serves 4–6

2¹/₄ pounds (1kg.) potatoes
1¹/₄ sticks (125g.) butter
salt and freshly ground black pepper
freshly grated nutmeg
2²/₃ cups (650ml.) heavy cream

Peel and slice your potatoes to the thickness of a nickel. Wash well in several changes of cold water to remove the starch, then pat dry.

Butter an ovenproof dish and put in a layer of potatoes. Season with salt, pepper and nutmeg, and dot with butter. Continue to add layers of potatoes, seasoning, and butter until the dish is half full, then pour on half the cream. Continue the process and then pour over the rest of the cream. Put into a medium oven under the roast and cook 1–1¹/₂ hours, depending on the heat of the oven (that is, if the roast is at 325°F (160°C), give the potatoes 1¹/₂ hours; if at 350–375°F (180–190°C), 1 hour).

greens

Greens come in all shapes and sizes, from the blandness of white cabbage to the sharpness of turnip tops. Without exception, they should be cooked to retain their texture. Gourmet stores may sell you *cime di rapa* (turnip or rape tops) or mustard greens in season, as well as the fashionable *cavolo nero*.

green beans with walnuts and garlic

This is a good way of livening up the dreariness of any beans you haven't picked fresh.

Serves 4

1/2 pound (225g.) green beans
salt
2 tablespoons olive oil
4 garlic cloves, cut into quarters
1/2 cup (50g.) shelled walnuts, cut into small pieces

Cook the beans in boiling salted water until *al dente*.

Heat the oil in a skillet and gently fry the garlic and walnuts for a few minutes.

Drain the beans and transfer to a serving dish, then pour the oil, garlic, and walnuts over them.

beet

beets with anchovy essence and fennel seeds

People eschew beets because they are somewhat messy, but rather than boil them, you can dry-roast them in the oven 40 minutes or so—or even cook them in the microwave before peeling them. Once they are cooked and peeled, you can do all sorts of things with them.

Cook 1 small beet per person. Put 6 small cooked beets in a saucepan with 1/3 cup (75ml.) white wine and 2 tablespoons of anchovy paste. Cover and cook over a medium heat 15 minutes. In a small skillet heat a little oil and cook a handful of fennel seeds until they pop. Put the beets in a serving dish, pour over the sauce, and sprinkle the seeds on top.

beets russian style

This is particularly good with boiled beef or with lamb.

Serves 4

1¹/2 pounds (700g.) small beets
2 tablespoons wine vinegar
4 small onions, sliced
1 cup (225ml.) beef stock
1 teaspoon caraway seeds
1/4 stick (25g.) butter
1 tablespoon plain flour
salt and freshly ground white pepper
1 teaspoon grated fresh horseradish
1/2 teaspoon superfine sugar
2 tablespoons sour cream

Cook and peel the beets and slice thinly. Put them in a non-metallic dish with the vinegar and set aside to marinate 30 minutes.

In a pan cook the onions in the stock with the caraway seeds until soft. Remove the onions from the stock and reserve. In a separate pan make a roux with the butter and flour, then add the stock and seeds to make a sauce. Simmer, stirring occasionally, 30 minutes.

Add the beets and their vinegar and the onions to the sauce. Season with salt, pepper, horseradish, and sugar, then spoon in the sour cream and stir well.

fennel

fennel with tomato and garlic

Fennel is a great aid to digestion and therefore good to serve with rich meat like pork or goose. It is easily cooked in a closed pan with butter, lemon juice, salt and pepper, and a little water about 30 minutes. (Belgian endive can be cooked the same way.) Here is an alternative treatment from that great book *Leaves From Our Tuscan Kitchen* by Janet Ross and Michael Wakefield. The first part can be done in advance, making this ideal for a dinner party.

Serves 4

4 fennel bulbs, trimmed, halved lengthwise and sliced
1/2 cup (125ml.) olive oil
1 onion, thinly sliced
4 garlic cloves, crushed
3/4 pound (350g.) tomatoes, skinned and coarsely chopped (or canned)
salt and freshly ground black pepper

Topping
1/2 cup (50g.) stale breadcrumbs
4 1/2 tablespoons (50g.) Parmesan, freshly grated
1 teaspoon finely grated lemon rind
1 garlic clove, chopped

Heat the oven to 425°F (220°C). In a pan heat the oil and fry the onion and garlic 2–3 minutes. Add the fennel and continue to fry, stirring occasionally with a wooden spoon. When the fennel is beginning to brown and is almost cooked, add the tomatoes and season with salt and pepper. Reduce the heat and cook 5 minutes. Transfer to a shallow gratin dish. Mix the topping ingredients together and spread over the fennel. Bake in the oven about 15 minutes until the top is crisp and golden brown.

parsnips

This is another vegetable that roasts well, but if you put parsnips in with the potatoes they will seldom be crispy unless they are charred. If you put them around the roast, however, they will do well and you can have the potatoes roasted separately.

I really like them best boiled and mashed with potato.

cabbage

braised white cabbage

This is the most delicious of vegetables, but one of the easiest to ruin. It has come back into favor with the restaurant scene cooked up with bacon, which is a natural partner. I actually like my cabbage quite plain and crunchy with a few caraway seeds. This recipe is from an anonymously published book by Prince Louis-Auguste de Bourbon, who describes it as "Italian style."

Serves 4–6

1 large white cabbage
1 bunch of scallions
4 garlic cloves
4 shallots
3 tablespoons chopped parsley
4 tablespoons oil
salt and freshly ground black pepper

Core and chop the cabbage and blanch it briefly in boiling water. Chop the scallions, cloves, and shallots. Sauté the scallions, garlic, shallots, and parsley in the oil, then add the cabbage and 2–3 tablespoons of water or stock. Season, cover, and simmer gently about 25 minutes.

braised red cabbage

This is the most neglected and tastiest of vegetables. It is best with dark meat or game, and actually benefits from being reheated. This is a Swedish recipe and must be gently cooked or it may burn.

Serves 6–8

1 large red cabbage, cored and shredded
1/2 stick (50g.) butter
2 tablespoons molasses
2 eating apples, peeled, cored and sliced
1 onion, grated
3 tablespoons lemon juice
1/2 cup (125ml.) red wine vinegar
salt

Melt the butter in a large heavy casserole, add the cabbage and molasses and stir well over a low heat 10 minutes. Add the apples, onion, lemon juice, vinegar, and some salt. Cover and simmer gently 2 hours.

leftovers

beef

cuban beef hash

In this instant age with its obsession with germs we have lost the joy of leftovers. It is one of the delights of a roast that with any luck there will be quite a lot left over. Even when I was young, a roast was meant to last from Sunday to Friday, which was of course a fish day. The old adage ran that you ate the meat hot on Sunday, cold on Monday (which was wash day) with pickles and chutney, and then you had leftovers on Tuesday and Wednesday and soup on Thursday. If you think of it like that, a roast is a very economical buy indeed. . I don't really expect you to follow that, but it is a fact that leftover dishes are delicious and usually pretty quick to make. All the ones I have provided are transferable to meats other than those given, so you can happily ring the changes, making additions as you go. I have left out fairly obvious ones like flans and pasta sauces because I'm sure you can work those out for yourselves. Make a stand against the throwaway world we have become, and make full use of your roast. Have fun and good eating.

There are many varieties of beef hash, and I have cooked most of them, but this Cuban dish is slightly unusual. It is generally served with rice, fried plantains, and fried eggs.

Serves 4–6

2¹/₄ pounds (1kg.) cooked beef, coarsely chopped
2 tablespoons oil
¹/₄ stick (25g.) butter
1 green and 1 red bell pepper, seeded and chopped
1 chili, seeded and chopped
1 large onion, finely chopped
3 garlic cloves, crushed
4 large tomatoes, peeled, seeded, and coarsely chopped
1 bay leaf
a large pinch of ground cloves
salt and freshly ground black pepper
1 tablespoon white wine vinegar

Heat the oil and butter in a large skillet, add the green and red bell peppers, the chili, onion, and garlic, and fry until the onion is golden. Add the tomatoes, bay leaf, and cloves, season with salt and pepper, and cook gently about 10 minutes. Add the vinegar and the meat and cook until the meat is heated through, stirring occasionally.

veeraswamy curry of cold meat

minced meat and lettuce curry

In 1924 an Indian gentleman by the name of Veeraswamy opened his restaurant on London's Regent Street. It quickly became the height of fashion, and when my Australian mother came as a bride to London in 1927 she was soon an ardent patron. I went there for the first time at the age of five, and I am happy to say it is still there and flourishing. Among the possessions that survived my wilderness years is Mr. Veeraswamy's *Indian Cookery*, a book I prefer above all others for Indian dishes. This very good dry curry can be done with any cold meat but I think it best with beef.

Serves 4

1 pound (500g.) cooked beef, cut into 1 inch (2.5cm) cubes
2 tablespoons (25g.) ghee or 3 tablespoons oil
2 tablespoons chopped onion
2 garlic cloves, chopped
3 chilies, sliced lengthwise
1/2 teaspoon peeled, chopped fresh ginger
2 teaspoons ground turmeric
1/2 teaspoon hot chili powder
salt
juice of 1/2 lemon

Warm the ghee or oil in a pan, then add the onion, garlic, chilies, and ginger. Cook until the onion is soft but not brown. Add the turmeric and chili powder, mix well, and cook 2–3 minutes. Add the meat, stir, and cook until the meat is warmed through. Add salt and lemon juice to taste. Serve with rice or Indian bread.

Another of Mr. Veeraswamy's specials—a double use of leftovers if you are overrun with bolting lettuce. Wash the lettuce and just shake dry, which will give you enough moisture.

Serves 2–3

1/2 pound (225g.) cooked beef, finely minced
1 small onion, finely chopped
1 garlic clove, finely chopped
2 tablespoons (25g.) ghee or 3 tablespoons oil
2 teaspoons ground coriander
1 teaspoon ground turmeric
1/2 teaspoon each chili powder, ground ginger, and ground cumin
1/2 teaspoon ground fenugreek
1 small lettuce, coarsely shredded
salt

Lightly fry the onion and garlic in the ghee or oil, then add the spices, and mix thoroughly. Cook 2–3 minutes, add the lettuce, and cook gently 10 minutes. Add the meat and salt to taste. Heat the meat through and serve.

sauté of beef père gaspard

Who Father Gaspard was, history doesn't relate, but this dish of recooked beef with chestnuts is delicious. Preferably buy chestnuts that are peeled and vacuum-packed (frozen are also available), although you can roast fresh nuts in a hot oven or boil them for easier peeling. Traditionally this dish is made with beef that has been potroasted or boiled.

Serves 4

1 pound (500g.) beef, cut into 1 inch (2.5cm.) cubes
1/4 stick (25g.) butter
3 onions, chopped
2 tablespoons all-purpose flour
2 cups (500ml.) hard cider
5 tablespoons beef stock
salt and freshly ground black pepper
1 bouquet garni (parsley, thyme, celery, bay leaf)
1 garlic clove, crushed
50 large chestnuts, peeled

Melt the butter in an ovenproof pan and soften the onions in the butter. Add the beef and brown on all sides. Remove the beef and onions from the pan and keep to one side. Add the flour to the fat remaining in the pan and cook this a few minutes to brown. Add the cider, stock, seasoning, bouquet garni, and garlic and cook, stirring, 10 minutes.

Place the chestnuts in the pan and cook, covered, 40 minutes, taking care not to break up the chestnuts when you stir the mixture.

Meanwhile, heat the oven to 350°F (180°C). Return the beef and onions to the pan and cook in the oven 20 minutes.

bubble and squeak

We think of this dish as just being made with greens and potatoes, but in the nineteenth century it was made with underdone cooked beef, lightly fried and well peppered. It was made without potatoes, but I have adapted it because I can't bear the thought!

Serves 8

1¹/2 pounds (700g.) each cooked shredded cabbage,
    cooked potatoes, coarsely chopped, and
    cooked beef, thinly sliced
1 cup (175g.) lard or 2 sticks butter
salt and freshly ground black pepper

Heat two thirds of the fat to a good heat in a large skillet. Mix the cabbage and potatoes together well and season. Put these into the pan and spread flat over the bottom. Fry briskly until the underside is crisp, then turn the mixture to fry the other side.

In a separate pan fry the meat slices gently in the remaining fat to heat them through. Pepper them well, twice what you think.

Transfer the potato mixture to a serving dish and arrange the beef on top. Serve with pickled walnuts or cucumber, or a butter sauce flavored with mustard, gherkins, and pickled onions.

lamb and mutton

alderman's walk

The Alderman's Walk is said to be the longest, largest cut from a haunch of mutton or venison that was reserved for Aldermen at City dinners in about the tenth century. As a member of the Butchers' Guild this makes total sense to me because the top table always get little special treats as rewards for their seniority, and quite right too. I am all for the rewards of earned privilege. In the nineteenth century, you would have exchanged the Worcestershire sauce for Harvey's and the Tabasco for chili sherry or cayenne, or both! Originally the mutton would have been cut from a freshly cooked roast slapped on the bread slices and left to cool so that the bread absorbed the juices before toasting.

Serves 4

4 slices of cooked mutton (3 ounces—75g each)
4 slices of good bread

Savory butter
1/2 stick (50g.) butter
1 heaped tablespoon chopped chives
2 tablespoons Worcestershire sauce
1 teaspoon (10g.) mustard
salt and freshly ground black pepper
Tabasco sauce

Soften the butter and mix with all the other savory butter ingredients. Cut the bread into strips and toast lightly. Cook the meat in the savory butter 8 minutes, turning once, then transfer to a serving dish. Pour over the butter, and arrange the toast around the dish.

to reheat a leg of lamb

This is a curious recipe from Elizabeth Ayrton, but one which works very well. It is a North Yorkshire recipe and therefore to be trusted.

Serves 6–8

1 leg of cold cooked lamb
salt and freshly ground black pepper
1 1/2 pounds (700g.) mashed potato, highly seasoned and allowed to cool
all-purpose flour seasoned with salt, black pepper, English mustard powder and cayenne pepper
dripping from the roast, supplemented with butter or margarine

Heat the oven to 400°F (200°C).

Rub salt and pepper into the carved surfaces of the meat, then press the potato into the hollow, and cover all the carved surface with it. Dredge the whole roast with seasoned flour and dot with fat. Put 4 tablespoons (55g.) fat into a roasting pan, place the roast in it, and roast in the oven 1 hour. Serve with mint sauce and gravy.

shepherd's pie

There is a great deal of nonsense talked about this excellent dish. It is not a rustic invention, but part of the post-industrial nostalgia for the countryside which was already raising its head in Victorian times, a sentimentality for a nonexistent world as later manifested by green boots and four-wheel drives among urban dwellers, and an aversion to field sports. Shepherd's pie came into the English cuisine after the Industrial Revolution when metal grinders for mincing became available, and is designed to use up cooked lamb or mutton. (If it is made with beef, it becomes cottage pie.) The version I have given was once again invented by my sister Heather, who used port or whiskey in the sauce.

Shepherd's pie can be made beforehand and finished off before serving. It freezes well.

Serves 6

2^{1}/$_{4}$ pounds (1kg.) cooked lamb
3 large strong onions, chopped
lard or vegetable oil for frying
^{1}/$_{4}$ stick (25g.) butter
4 tablespoons (25g.) all-purpose flour
1^{1}/$_{4}$ cups (300ml.) meat stock
^{2}/$_{3}$ cup (50ml.) port or whisky (or use milk if preferred)
salt and freshly ground black pepper

Potato topping
2^{1}/$_{4}$ pounds (1kg.) potatoes, peeled
75g butter
a little milk

Grind the lamb. Gently fry the onions in a little fat until pale golden and soft, then drain well.

Make a roux in a saucepan with the butter and flour and cook 2 minutes, then slowly add the stock and other liquid to make a smooth but fairly thick sauce. Remove from the heat and mix in the meat and onions. Season well (a dash of Worcestershire sauce is a good addition) and cook over a low heat about 3 minutes. Transfer the meat mixture to a shallow ovenproof dish and leave to cool.

Heat the oven to 350°F (180°C).

For the topping, boil the potatoes in salted water until tender, then drain, and leave to steam dry. Mash well with half the butter, a good amount of seasoning, and a little milk (they want to be stiff).

Spread the potatoes at least 1 inch (2.5cm.) thick over the meat, and score the top with a fork (Victorian versions say "like a ploughed field!"). Dot the potato with the remaining butter and cook in the oven 40 minutes. The top should be golden brown.

lamb moussaka

This is a classic dish of the Aegean. When I was on a charter yacht in Greece I couldn't get the cook to make it, and I have never eaten it in Greece, although I have in Turkey and in Greek restaurants over here. It is also known as Greek shepherd's pie, which is unlikely as Greek shepherds live rather primitively in the hills without ovens— but it is delicious none the less!

Serves 6–8

2^1/4 pounds (1kg.) cooked lamb, minced
1 cup (225ml.) olive oil
1^1/2 pounds (700g.) zucchini, sliced lengthwise ^{1}/3 inch
  (1cm.) thick
1 pound (500g.) eggplant, prepared as the zucchini
^{3}/4 stick (75g.) butter
1 large onion, finely chopped
1 garlic clove, finely chopped
3 tomatoes, skinned, seeded, and chopped
salt and freshly ground black pepper
5 tablespoons dry breadcrumbs
4 tablespoons chopped parsley
2 cups (500ml.) White Sauce (see page 130)
3 eggs, beaten
^{1}/2 pound (250g.) ricotta or cottage cheese
^{1}/2 cup (75g.) Parmesan cheese, freshly grated
1 pound (500g.) potatoes, sliced and parboiled

Heat the oil in a large skillet and fry the zucchini and eggplant until lightly browned. Transfer to paper towels to drain. Add ^{1}/2 stick (50g.) of the butter to the pan, and sauté the onion and garlic until golden. Add the lamb, tomatoes, and some salt and pepper, cover, and cook 10 minutes. Remove from the heat and add half the breadcrumbs and all the parsley.

Heat the oven to 375°F (90°C).

Prepare the White Sauce, and stir in the beaten eggs and both the cheeses.

Use the remaining butter to grease a large baking dish. Sprinkle the dish with the remaining breadcrumbs. Put in a layer of potato slices, then half the meat mixture, then a layer of eggplant, the remaining meat mixture, and finally the zucchini. Top with the White Sauce and bake in the oven about 45 minutes or until golden brown and sizzling.

dormers

In the same way that the West Indians call goat by the name of the more expensive mutton, so these little lamb or mutton rissoles are said to represent the more expensive dormouse, which takes the dish back to Roman times.

Makes 20

1^1/$_3$ pounds (600g.) cooked lamb or mutton
^{3}/$_4$ cup (125g.) onion, finely chopped
^{1}/$_4$ pound (125g.) suet, finely chopped (use chilled butter, coarsely grated, if you have an aversion to suet)
1 cup (250g.) cooked long-grain rice
salt and freshly ground black pepper
4 eggs, beaten
some stale breadcrumbs
vegetable oil or fat for frying

Chop the meat finely or put through a meat grinder, and mix with the onions, suet, and rice, then season to taste with salt and pepper. Bind with 2 of the beaten eggs and mold into little sausage shapes of about 3 tablespoons (50g.) each. Coat with the remaining 2 beaten eggs, roll in the breadcrumbs, and shallow-fry until golden brown.

lamb and endive

In this recipe I do mean endive— frisée, the curly salad vegetable—and not chicory, although you could use that instead.

Serves 4

1 pound (500g.) cold cooked lamb, thinly sliced
2–3 heads of endive, cored

Tomato sauce
2^1/$_4$ pound (1kg.) tomatoes, skinned and chopped (use canned out of season or for ease and economy)
^{1}/$_4$ stick (25g.) butter
1 celery stalk, diced
1 onion, sliced
1 tablespoon olive oil
salt

For the tomato sauce, melt the butter in a medium pan and cook the celery and onion until softened. Add the tomatoes, oil, and some salt, and simmer 30 minutes until the sauce has thickened. Strain the sauce and adjust the seasoning. Return to the pan.

Bring a separate saucepan of water to a boil and cook the endives 5 minutes after the water returns to a boil. Squeeze out all the moisture and chop finely.

Add the endive to the tomato sauce, then place the lamb on top and reheat without allowing the sauce to boil. Transfer to a serving dish.

veal

dunelmo of veal

A good dish for lunch or supper, to be served on toast.

Serves 4–6

1 pound (500g.) cooked veal, minced
$^1/_4$ stick (25g.) butter
1 ounce (25g.) mushrooms, finely chopped
$1^1/_2$ tablespoons all-purpose flour
$^1/_3$ cup (75ml.) heavy cream
salt and freshly ground black pepper

Lightly brown the veal in the butter, add the mushrooms and fry gently a few minutes. Stir in the flour, add the cream, and season with salt and pepper. Simmer 3–4 minutes and serve.

inveresk veal

An invention I flung together while cooking veal for this book. It can also be done with a veal chop.

Serves 4

8 slices of cooked veal
1 tablespoon olive oil
2 teaspoons (10g.) butter
3 onions, chopped
4 canned anchovy fillets
1 tablespoon Dijon mustard
$^1/_3$ cup (75ml.) white wine

Heat the oil and butter in a large skillet and fry the onions until pale golden. Add the anchovies and mustard and cook together until they blend in. Add the meat and cook lightly, turning them to brown. Pour on the wine and cook a further 3–4 minutes. Serve with the pan juices.

dowlet pie

pork

pork puffs

This is a London dish of leftover veal that I suspect has medieval and Crusader origins.

Serves 4–6

1¹/₂ pounds (700g.) cooked veal, chopped
2 sticks (200g.) butter (beef suet in the original), diced
8 plums or soaked prunes, or 1 cup (175g.) muscat raisins
8 dates
²/₃ cup (150ml.) white wine
a little sugar
a handful of sage leaves
a pinch of dried thyme
a pinch each of grated nutmeg and ground cinnamon
³/₄ stick (75g.) butter

Heat the oven to 350°F (180°C).

Layer the veal, 1¹/₄ sticks (125g.) butter, the plums or prunes or raisins, and dates in an ovenproof pie dish, sprinkling each layer with a little sugar and the herbs and spices. Moisten with most of the wine and bake in the oven 35–40 minutes.

Boil the remaining wine, sugar, and butter together and pour over the veal dish before serving.

A good way of dealing with cold pork, or indeed any cold meat.

Makes 6

1 pack phyllo pastry
about ¹/₂ stick (50g.) butter, melted

Filling
¹/₄ pound (125g.) cooked pork, finely chopped
1 cooked potato, chopped
2–3 sun-dried tomatoes, chopped
2 sprigs of oregano, chopped
1 teaspoon chutney
salt and freshly ground black pepper

Heat the oven to 400°F (200°C).

Mix all the filling ingredients together, seasoning to taste with salt and pepper. Lay out a sheet of phyllo pastry and brush with melted butter. Add another sheet on top, brush with melted butter and repeat again. Put a spoonful of filling in the middle and fold over to form a package. Brush the edges with melted butter and put on a baking sheet, seam-side down. Repeat until all the mixture is used up. You should get about six oblong packages. Bake in the oven about 8–10 minutes until golden brown.

pork crêpes

Everyone likes a pancake and this is a good way of using up cold meat. Pancakes can be frozen as made, with paper between them to keep them separate, for a really quick supper dish.

Serves 4

8 thin slices of cooked pork
3–4 shallots, finely sliced
3/4 stick (75g.) butter
2 teaspoons Dijon mustard
1/2 cup (125ml.) dry vermouth
2/3 cup (150ml.) double cream, whisked
2 tablespoons (25g.) Parmesan, freshly grated

Crêpes
1 cup (110g.) all-purpose flour
a pinch of salt
3 eggs, beaten
1 1/4 cups (300ml.) milk
3/4 stick (75g.) butter, melted

To make the crêpes, put the flour and salt in a bowl, make a well in the center, then add the eggs, then the milk. Beat from the center outward until you have a smooth batter. Stir in the melted butter. Make the pancakes in a small, non-stick pan in the usual way, and set aside. The batter should yield between 8 and 12 crêpes.

Heat the oven to 400°F (200°C).

Sauté the shallots in 1/2 stick (50g.) of the butter until soft, then stir in the mustard, and mix well. Add the vermouth, bring to a boil, reduce the heat and cook until the mixture is thick.

Lay a slice of meat on each crêpe, then anoint with the shallot mixture. Add a dollop of cream and a sprinkle of cheese. Roll up and lay in a buttered gratin dish. Sprinkle with the remaining cheese, dot with the remaining butter, and bake in the oven 15 minutes.

hot spicy pork

I have slightly altered this dish from one in Sri Owen's *Rice Book*. Sri was one of my favorite cooks, and I never missed her book signings with tastings when I was in London.

Serves 6

1^1/$_2$ pounds (700g.) cooked pork, cut into 1 inch
   (2.5cm.) cubes
4 tablespoons oil
1 large onion, chopped
1 tablespoon white wine vinegar
2 ripe tomatoes, skinned, seeded and chopped
salt and freshly ground black pepper
^{1}/$_2$ cup (125ml.) hot water

Paste
1 small onion, chopped
2 garlic cloves, chopped
2–3 large red chilies, chopped
1 teaspoon each chopped peeled fresh root ginger
   and ground coriander
^{1}/$_2$ teaspoon each ground cumin, turmeric,
   cinnamon, and sugar mixed
1 tablespoon white wine vinegar
2 tablespoons hot water

Process all the paste ingredients together in a food processor. Heat the oil in a wok or frying pan and stir-fry the pork 5 minutes. Remove the pork and set aside. Fry the onion in the same oil 2–3 minutes, then add the paste, and stir-fry a further 2–3 minutes. Return the pork to the pan and add the vinegar and tomatoes. Stir, cover, and cook 3 minutes. Adjust the seasoning, add the water, and simmer, uncovered, a final 15 minutes. Serve with cooked rice.

pork chow mein

Chow mein, like chop suey, is a westernized Chinese invention, but none the worse for that. It is an excellent use for cold pork. You can really add anything to it, but here is a basic recipe. After that, use your imagination.

Serves 4

^{3}/$_4$ pound (350g.) cooked pork
2 tablespoons oil (sesame for authenticity)
1 bunch of scallions, chopped
^{1}/$_4$ pound (125g.) beansprouts (or a can, drained)
3 tablespoons soy sauce
2 tablespoons cornstarch
1^2/$_3$ cups (425ml.) stock
a pinch of five-spice powder (optional)
1 package ramen noodles (or other egg noodles)

Cut the meat into thin strips. Heat the oil in a wok or deep skillet, add the scallions and cook 3 minutes. Add the beansprouts and soy sauce and cook a further 2 minutes. Mix the cornstarch and stock together until smooth and pour over the vegetables. Add the five-spice powder, if using, bring to a boil, stirring well, then lower the heat and cook 3 minutes.

Cook the noodles according to the package instructions. Mix into the vegetable mixture with the meat, heat through, and transfer to a warmed serving dish.

ham

gratin of ham and belgian endive (or leek) rolls

This combination of ham with cheese and leeks is one of my favorites. It is total comfort food to me and, living alone, I get the dish to scrape... Yes!

Serves 6

6 slices cooked ham
6 heads Belgian endive (or 6 leeks)
salt
2^1/$_2$ cups (600ml.) White Sauce (see page 130)
1^1/$_2$ cups (175g.) strong Cheddar cheese, grated
1 teaspoon each English mustard powder and
   cayenne pepper
butter for greasing

Heat the oven to 400°F (200°C).

If using endive remove the core. (If using leeks, trim them, cutting off most of the green.) Put the vegetables into salted boiling water and cook 5 minutes. Drain well.

Heat the White Sauce and melt two thirds of the cheese into it. Stir in the mustard powder and cayenne.

Carefully wrap the ham slices around the chicory or leeks, and place in a buttered ovenproof dish. Pour over the sauce, scatter on the rest of the cheese, and bake in the oven 30 minutes until the sauce is bubbling and the top golden.

ham, parsnip, and walnut fritters

The late great Jane Grigson gave a lovely recipe for these fritters, but I couldn't resist adding ham to them.

Serves 6

^{1}/$_4$ pound (100g.) cooked ham, finely chopped
2^1/$_4$ pounds (1kg.) parsnips
2 large eggs, beaten
^{2}/$_3$ cup (150ml.) milk
1–2 tablespoons all-purpose flour
^{3}/$_4$ stick (75g.) butter, melted
salt and freshly ground black pepper
^{3}/$_4$ cup (100g.) shelled walnuts, chopped
vegetable oil for deep-frying

Peel and trim the parsnips and cook in a pan of boiling water until soft, then drain, and purée them. Mix to a smooth paste with the eggs, milk, flour, and melted butter. Season with salt and pepper, then stir in the ham and walnuts.

Heat a deep pan of oil to 350–375°F (180–190°C). Mold the ham mixture into fritters about the size of half a biscuit, and cook in the hot oil until golden, about 10 minutes. Drain well on paper towels.

molded ham soufflé

This is a delicious way of using up ham. A molded soufflé always looks attractive and tastes great. It is a good supper-party dish.

Serves 6

10 ounces (300g.) cooked ham
$^1/_2$ cup (125ml.) brandy
$1^1/_4$ cups (300ml.) White Sauce (see page 130)
$^1/_4$ stick (25g.) clarified butter, melted
$2^1/_2$ tablespoons (15g.) all-purpose flour
4 tablespoons freshly grated Parmesan cheese
4 eggs, separated
salt and freshly ground black pepper
freshly grated nutmeg

Cut half the ham into small pieces and marinate in the brandy 2 hours.

Heat the oven to 400°F (200°C). Chop the remaining ham very finely and add it to the White Sauce. Mix the ham and sauce well, then add the melted butter, flour, 3 tablespoons Parmesan, the egg yolks, marinated ham, and brandy. Mix very well and season with salt, pepper, and a pinch of nutmeg.

Beat the egg whites until very stiff, then fold them into the ham mixture with a metal spoon. Transfer to a buttered 9-inch (23cm.) soufflé dish which you have sprinkled with the remaining grated Parmesan. Set this in a large roasting pan of water so that the water comes halfway up the soufflé dish. Bake in the oven 45–50 minutes. Remove from the oven and the water, leave to cool for 10 minutes, then serve.

poultry

shaker chicken pudding

The Shakers were a curious sect which originated in England in around the eighteenth century, and they were driven out of the country because of alleged sexual impropriety. They settled in America where they formed farming communities and made exquisite furniture. The chairs, which were designed to be hung on the walls during community dancing, are particularly fine. The name "Shakers" described the shaking movements used during communal worship.

Serves 4–6

1 pound (500g.) cooked chicken meat, diced
1 apple, peeled, cored, and diced
1 onion, chopped
1 celery stalk, chopped
1 stick (100g.) butter
1/2 cup (125ml.) hard cider
salt and freshly ground black pepper
freshly grated nutmeg
1 cup (100g.) dry breadcrumbs

Sauce
1/4 stick (25g.) butter
1 tablespoon all-purpose flour
2/3 cup (175ml.) heavy cream

Sauté the apple, onion, and celery in 1/2 stick (50g.) of the butter until soft. Add the cider and salt, pepper, and nutmeg to taste. Simmer, covered, 30 minutes until the vegetables are soft. Continue to cook, uncovered, until the mixture reduces a little.

Preheat the oven to 350°F (180°C).

For the sauce, make a roux with the butter and flour, then add the cream and cook, stirring, until it thickens.

Mix the cooked vegetable hash and the chicken into the cream sauce. Pour into a buttered ovenproof dish, sprinkle with the breadcrumbs, and dot with the remaining butter. Bake in the oven 20 minutes.

chicken croquettes

This is a wonderful stand-by, and you can ring the changes with all sorts of different additions and sauces.

Makes about 14

14 ounces (400g.) cooked chicken meat, finely chopped
2 teaspoons (10g.) butter
2 tablespoons all-purpose flour, plus extra for dusting
2/3 cup (175ml.) mixed chicken stock and heavy cream
2 egg yolks
1/2 cup (75g.) red bell pepper, seeded and chopped
1/3 cup (50g.) capers, chopped
salt and freshly ground black pepper
1 large egg, beaten
stale breadcrumbs
vegetable oil for frying

Make a roux with the butter and flour, then slowly stir in the stock/cream mixture and cook until thick and smooth. Reduce the heat and cook a further 2 minutes. Beat in the egg yolks, then stir in the chicken, red bell pepper, and capers, and some salt and pepper to taste. Let cool.

Put the extra flour, beaten egg, and breadcrumbs on separate plates. Form the chicken mixture into oblong shapes about 2 inches (5cm.) in diameter and dip first in the flour, then in the egg, then in the breadcrumbs. Fry in hot oil for about 6–8 minutes, or until golden brown and heated through. Serve with a simple tomato sauce.

potted turkey

I am fond of cold turkey, so I don't have a problem after Christmas. Most recooked turkey dishes are pretty nasty, so any I don't eat cold I strip from the carcass and pot. This is very useful for sandwiches or as an appetizer, and freezes beautifully.

Serves 8–10 as an appetizer

2 1/4 pounds (1kg.) cooked turkey, both light and dark meat, skin and tendons removed
3 1/2 sticks (350g.) butter
juice of 2 lemons
cayenne pepper
freshly grated nutmeg
salt and freshly ground black pepper

Put the turkey into a food processor and grind it 2 minutes. Melt the butter and add half of it to the turkey, along with the lemon juice and the seasonings (use plenty of nutmeg). Put into a dish and pour the rest of the butter over the top. Let cool.

turkey turnovers

fish

salmon fish cakes

This American dish can be made with any poultry and most leftover meats.

Serves 6

Filling
1/2 pound (250g.) cooked turkey, white and dark meat, chopped
1 tablespoon each finely chopped parsley and chives
2 tablespoons each finely chopped small white onions and green bell pepper
1/2 cup (125ml.) turkey gravy
2 tablespoons dry sherry
1 egg yolk
2 tablespoons heavy cream
salt and freshly ground black pepper

Dough
2 1/4 cups (225g.) all-purpose flour
a pinch of salt
2 sticks (200g.) unsalted butter
1/2–1 cup (100–225ml.) iced water

Mix the dough ingredients into a firm dough and rest for 30 minutes. Preheat the oven to 400°F (200°C).

Roll out the dough on a floured board to an oblong of about 12 x 8 inches (30 x 20cm.) and cut into six 4 inch (10cm.) squares. Mix all the turkey filling ingredients together except the egg yolk and cream, and check the seasoning. Put 1 tablespoon turkey mix on each square of dough and fold over. Seal the edges with water. Mix the egg yolk and cream together and brush the turnovers with it. Bake in the oven 15 minutes or until golden brown. Serve at once.

I have always found fish cakes awfully bland. The average one is a blend of fish and potato with not a lot of flavour. But then some time in the 1980s I thought, why am I doing this—you can put other things in as well. Since then I have used smoked fish, laverbread, chopped hard-boiled eggs, chopped capers and scallions to liven up my fishcakes. I am particularly fond of using half white potato and half sweet potato to avoid the gluey effect, and there is of course Jane Grigson's fishcake in *Good Things* which is bound with a white sauce.

Makes about 16

1 pound (500g.) cooked salmon, flaked
1/2 pound (250g.) potatoes
1/2 pound (250g.) sweet potatoes
1 bunch of scallions, finely chopped
2 eggs
salt and freshly ground black pepper
vegetable oil for frying

Boil your potatoes, drain and mash well. If you are using white sweet potatoes rather than the orange ones, they will take twice as long to cook as an ordinary "Irish potato."

Mix together the mashed potato with everything else, except the oil, all of which can be done in a food processor. Form into small cakes about the size of half a biscuit and chill 30 minutes. Fry in the hot oil until golden brown. Fish cakes can be cooked in the oven but are never so good. Fish cakes freeze well.

salmon rillettes

We all know pork rillettes, which we eat with more or less delight on vacation in France. Try salmon rillettes: They are quite delicious.

Serves 6–8

¹/₂ pound (250g.) cooked salmon, flaked
1³/₄ sticks (175g.) butter, softened
salt and freshly ground black pepper
juice of 1 lemon

Mix the salmon and butter together in a bowl, trying not to break up the fish too much. Season well and mix in the lemon juice. Store in small ramekins.

cold salmon mousse

Salmon mousse comes in many forms. This one is a great favorite in my home.

Serves 6

2¹/₄ pounds (1kg.) cooked salmon
4 egg whites, 2 unbeaten and 2 stiffly beaten
³/₄ cup (200ml.) heavy cream
salt and freshly ground black pepper

Heat the oven to 350°F (180°C).

In a food processor or pestle and mortar blend the salmon to a paste, adding the 2 unbeaten egg whites. Remove to a bowl and beat in the cream and the stiffly beaten whites. Season to taste. Place in a buttered 9 inch (23cm.) mold and poach in a bain-marie in the oven 40–45 minutes or until set and firm.

Remove from the oven and stand 5 minutes before unmolding. Serve with Tomato Sauce (see page 146).

kedgeree

I often think of the Memsahib who invented kedgeree. Was she poor and making ends meet? Was her husband a tyrant, or did she do it to please? Or was she just bored? Who knows—but whatever the story, we owe her a debt of gratitude. I tend to make my kedgeree with smoked haddock and keep it simple, but with cooked salmon you need a little more flavor. The dish originated from the Indian "khichiri," a dish of rice and lentils, and the recipe I have given is more in keeping with that. It is a great dish whatever way you prepare it. To bulk out the recipe, you can add cauliflower or potatoes.

Serves 8

1 pound (500g.) cooked salmon, flaked
1 teaspoon coriander seeds
1/2 teaspoon cardamom seeds
1 tablespoon ground turmeric
1 teaspoon cayenne pepper
1 dried red chili
4 tablespoons ghee or clarified butter
1 onion, 1/2 roughly chopped, 1/2 slivered
2 1/3 cups (500g.) long-grain rice
2 1/3 cups (500g.) brown lentils
salt
4 hard-boiled eggs, shelled and cut into quarters
1 tablespoon vegetable oil
1 tablespoon slivered almonds

Pound the spices and chili together. Put them in a saucepan with a generous quart (1.2 liters) water and simmer 10 minutes. Strain and keep the water.

In a large saucepan melt the ghee or butter and fry the chopped onion until colored. Add the rice and lentils and cook, stirring continuously, 2 minutes. Add the strained spice water and the salt and simmer until all the moisture has been absorbed and all is cooked and tender. Stir in the cooked fish carefully along with the hard-boiled eggs.

Heat the oil in a separate pan and fry the onion slivers until brown and crisp, then drain well on kitchen paper. Sauté the almonds quickly. Turn the kedgeree into a serving dish and put the onions and almonds over the top. Serve as is, or with a curry sauce if liked.

meat suppliers

Here are the websites of some good suppliers of meat.

Lobel's
www.lobels.com

Niman Ranch
www.nimanranch.com

Allen Brothers
www.allenbrothers.com

Uptown Prime
www.order-steaks.com

My Butcher
www.mybutcher.com

Prather Ranch
www.pratherranch.com

Harris Ranch
www.harrisranchbeef.com

John's Meat Market
www.johnsmarket.com

These are meat suppliers that also specialize in Game. Game is increasingly available in grocery stores and meat markets.
You can ask your butcher to order it for you or look in the Yellow Pages under "meats". Alternatively you can use mail order. Here are some suppliers that may be of help.

888 Eat Game
Tel: 888-EAT-GAME
www.888eatgame.com
Retail and wholesale meats from alligator to zebra

Broadleaf Venison USA, Inc.
3050 East 11th Street
Los Angeles
California 90023
Tel: 800-336-3844
www.broadleafgame.com
Wholesale and mail order

Broken Arrow Ranch
P.O. Box 530
Ingram
Texas 78025
Tel: 800-962-4263
www.brokenarrowranch.com
Wholesale and mail order

D'Artagnan Inc.
399 St. Paul Avenue
Jersey City
New Jersey 07306
Tel: 800-327-8246
Wholesale and mail order

Durham Meat Company
P.O. Box 26158
San Jose
California 95159
Tel: 800-233-8742
Wholesale and mail order

ExoticMeats.com
Tel: 800-680-4375
www.exoticmeats.com

Hills Foods Ltd.
109-3650 Bonneville Place
Burnaby
British Columbia
Canada
V3N 4T7
Tel: 604-421-3100
www.hillsfoods.com
Wholesale only

Game Sales International
2456 E. 13th Street
P.O. Box 7719
Loveland
CO 80537
Tel: 800-729-2090
www.gamesalesintl.com

Joie DeVivre
P.O. Box 875
Modesto
California 95353
Tel: 800-648-8854
Mail order

MacFarlane Pheasant Farm, Inc.
2821 South U.S. Hwy. 51
Janesville
Wisconsin 53546
Tel: 800-345-8348
Wholesale and mail order

Mount Royal USA Inc.
3902 N Main
Houston
Texas 77009
Tel: 800-730-3337
www.mountroyal.com

Musicon Farms
157 Scotchtown Road
Goshen
New York 10924
Tel: 914-294-6378
Wholesale and mail order

Native Game
12556 WCR 21/2
Brighton
Colorado 80601
Tel: 800-952-6321
Wholesale and mail order

Nicky USA, Inc.
223 S.E. 3rd Avenue
Portland
Oregon 97214
Tel: 800-469-4162
www.nickyusa.com
Wholesale and mail order

Nightbird
358 Shaw Road
South San Francisco
California 94080
Tel: 650-737-5876
Wholesale and mail order

Polaricia (Wholesale)/The Game
Exchange (Retail)
P.O. Box 990204
San Francisco
California 94124
Tel: 800-GAME-USA
Wholesale and retail

Prairie Harvest
P.O. Box 1013
Spearfish
South Dakota 57783
Tel: 800-350-7166
Wholesale and mail order

The Sausage Maker, Inc.
1500 Clinton Street, Bldg. 123
Buffalo
New York 14206
Tel: 716-824-6510
www.sausagemaker.com
Wholesale and mail order

Valley Game & Gourmet
P.O. Box 2713
Salt Lake City
Utah 84110
www.valleygame.com

notes

suppliers

notes

index